Some Pages Inside

I0465748

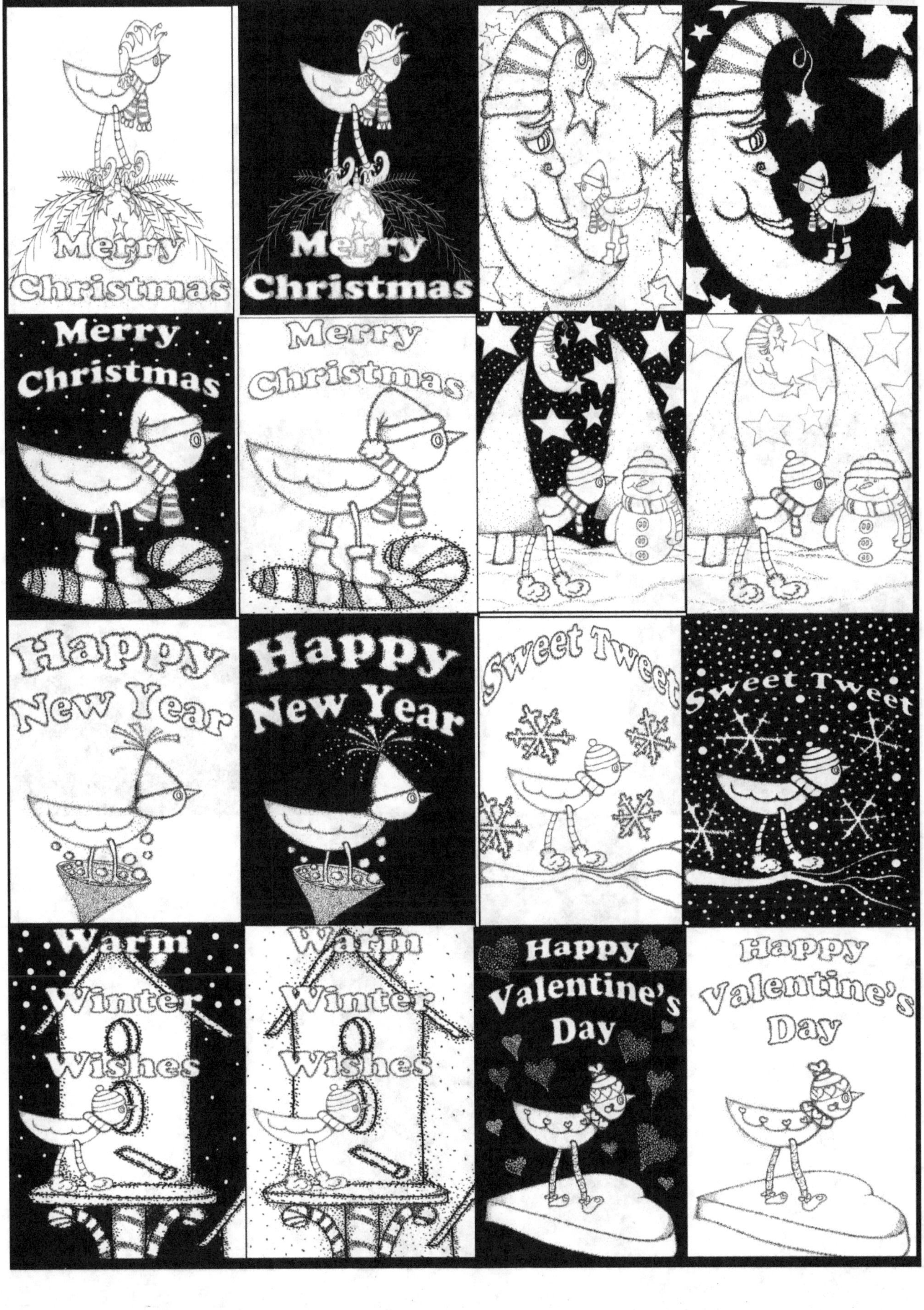

Merry Christmas

Merry Christmas

Merry Christmas

Merry Christmas

Happy New Year

Happy New Year

Sweet Tweet

Sweet Tweet

Warm Winter Wishes

Warm Winter Wishes

Happy Valentine's Day

Happy Valentine's Day

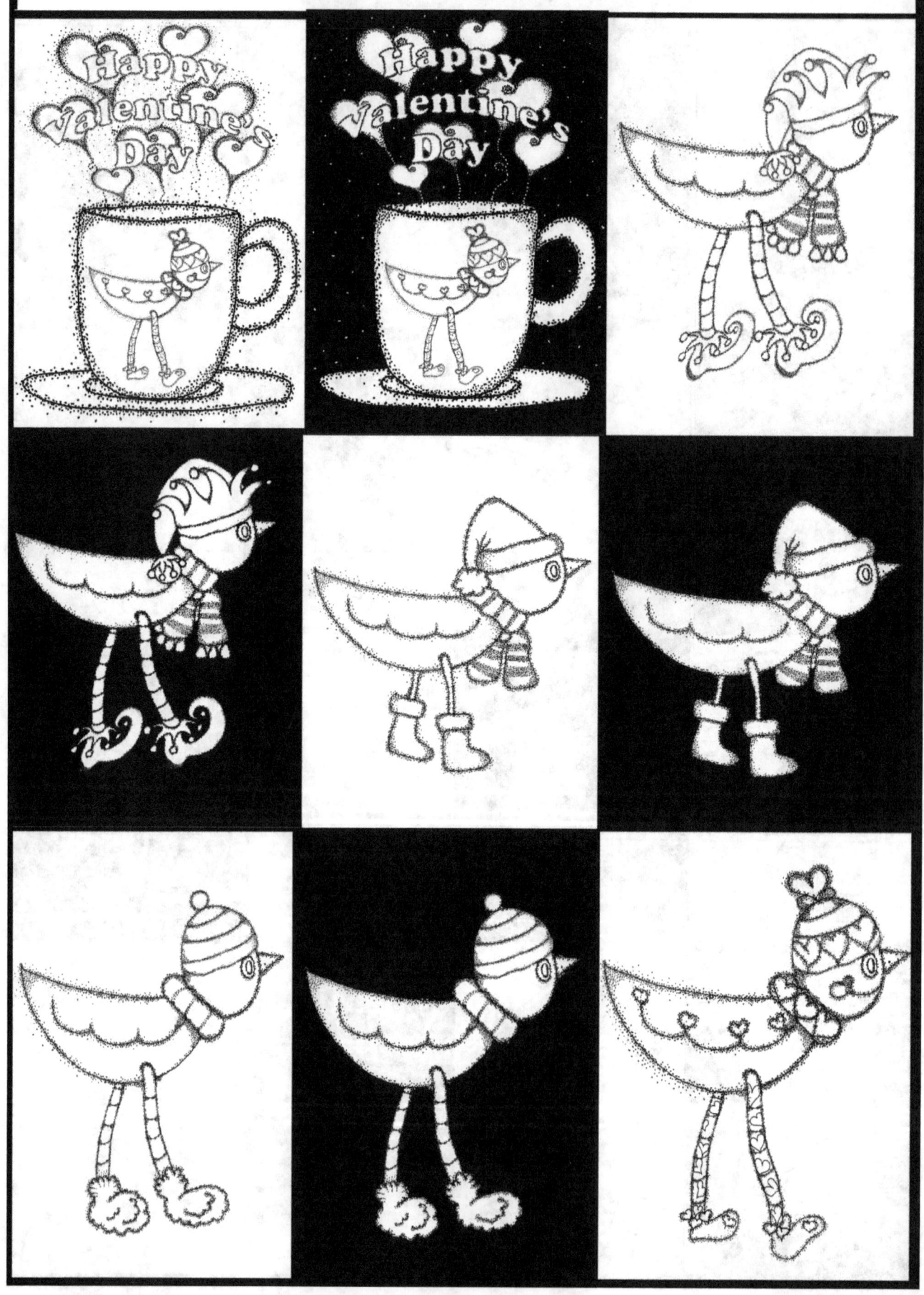

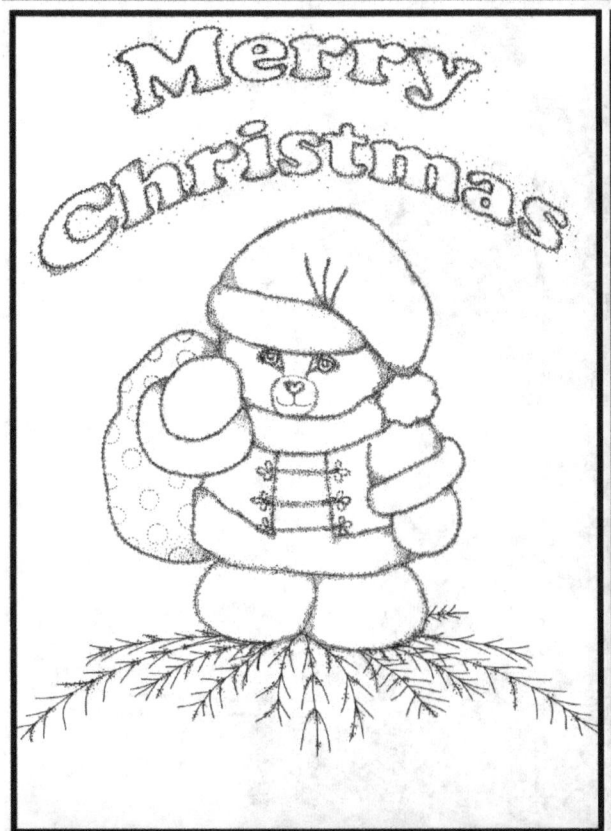

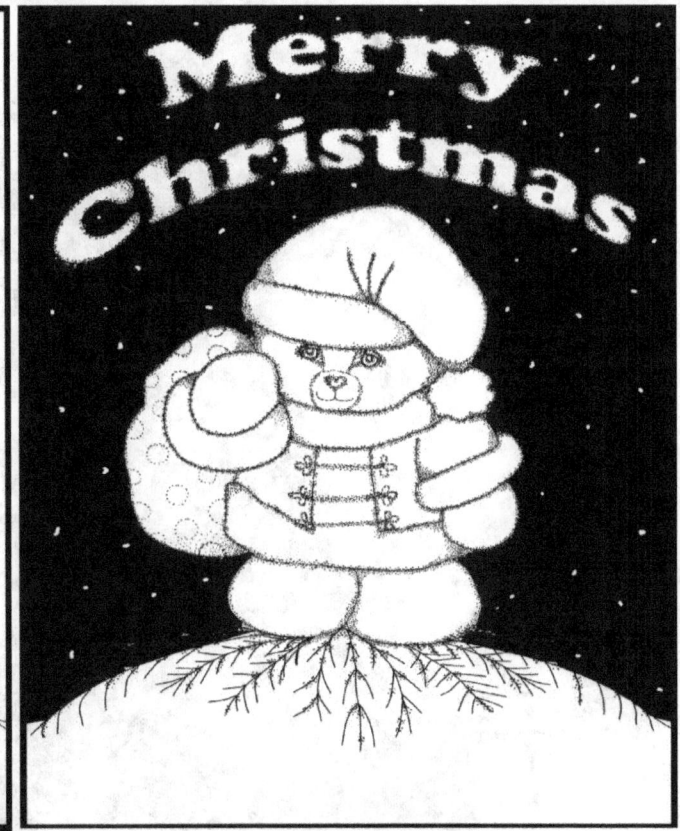

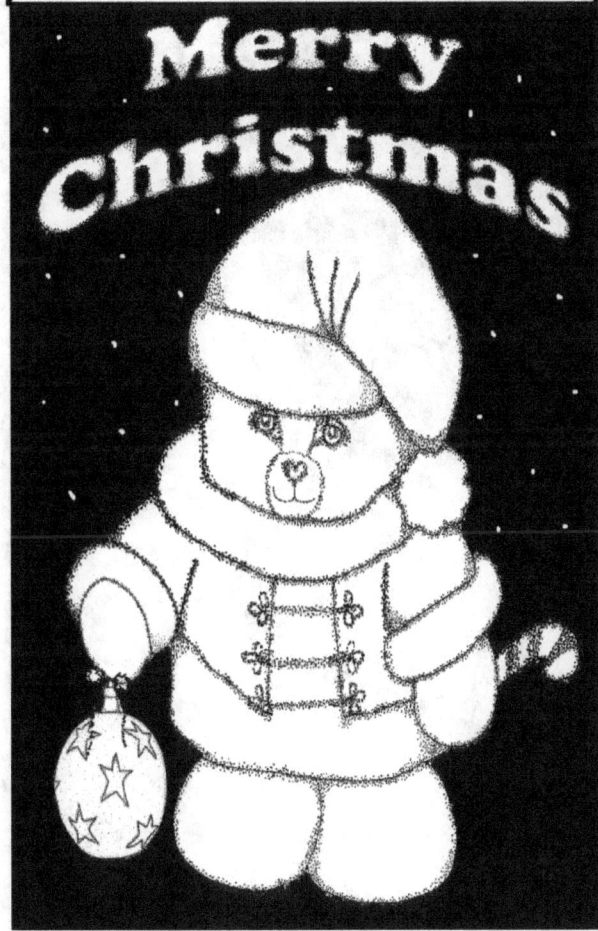

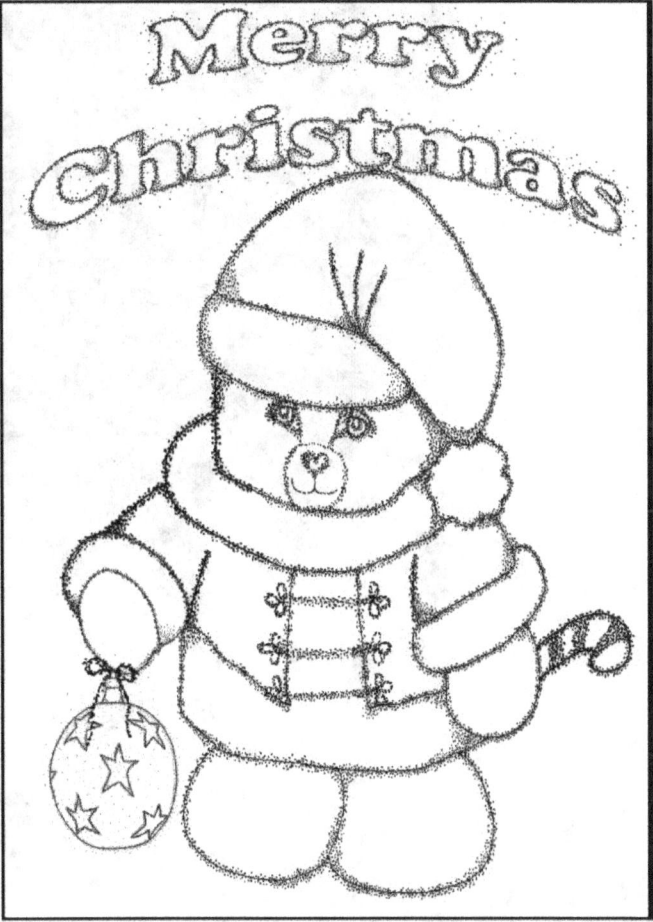

Welcome To Sweet Tweet & Buddy Bear's Winter Coloring Book

all art is protected by copyright law ©J mcdonald designs 2018

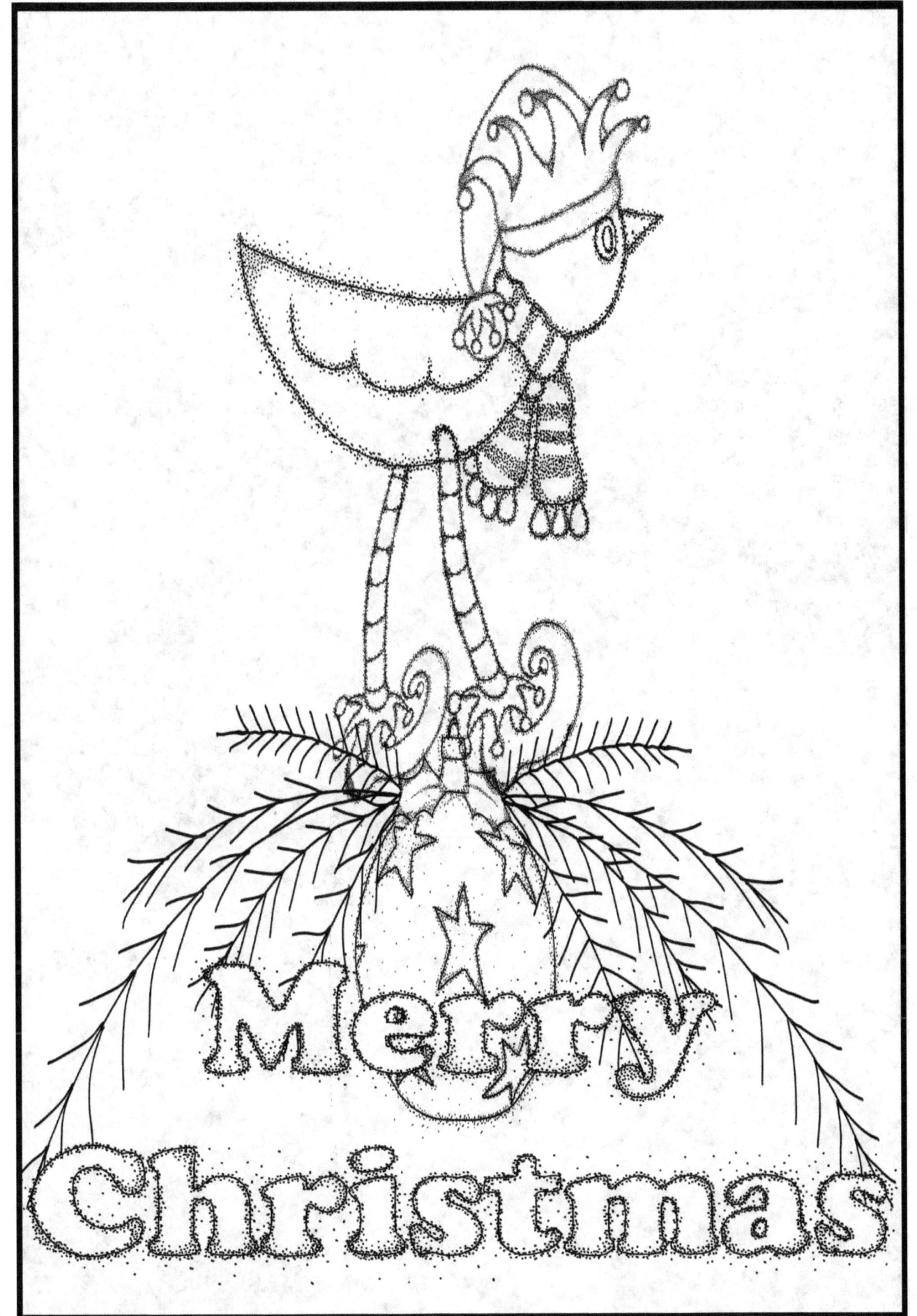

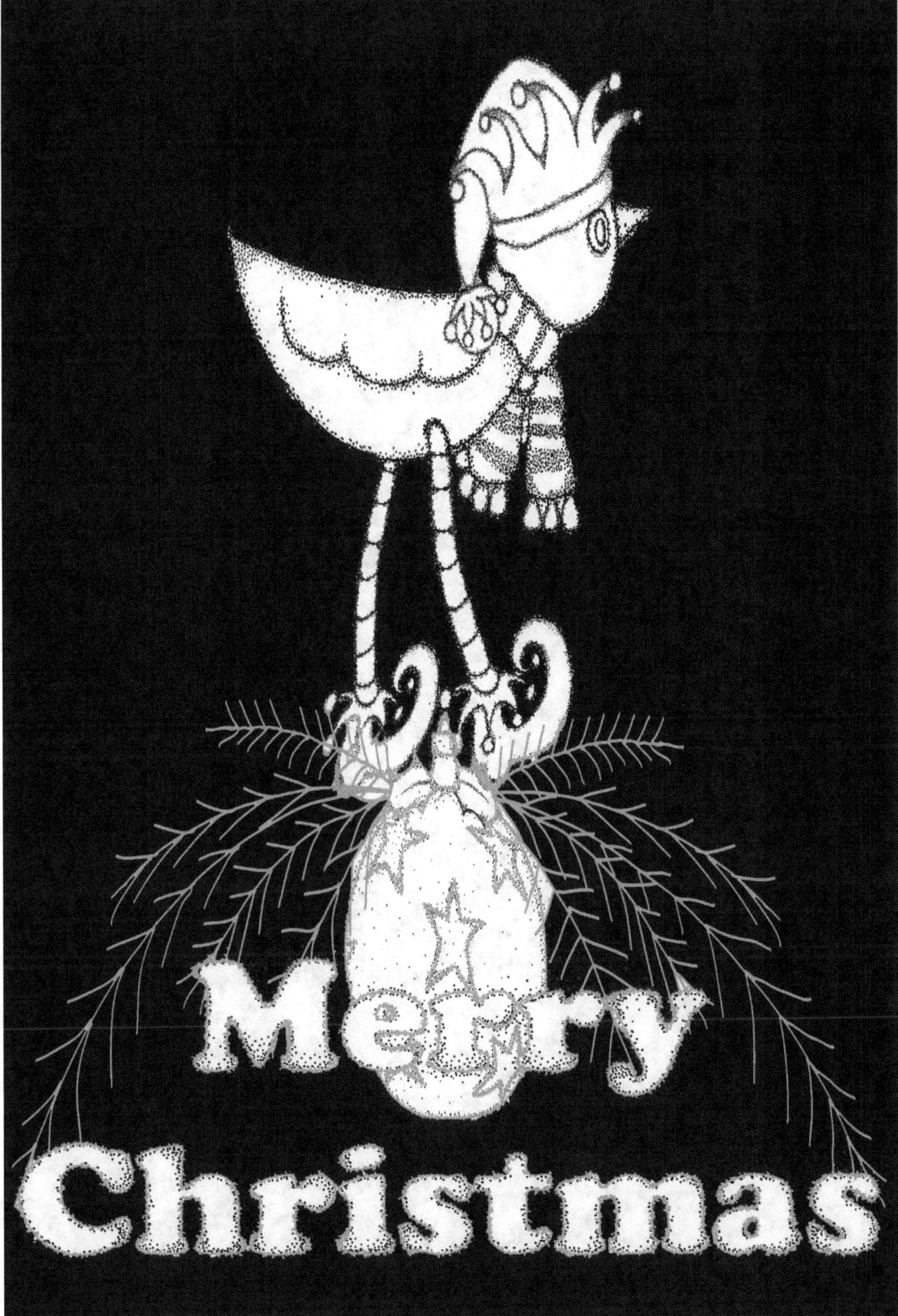

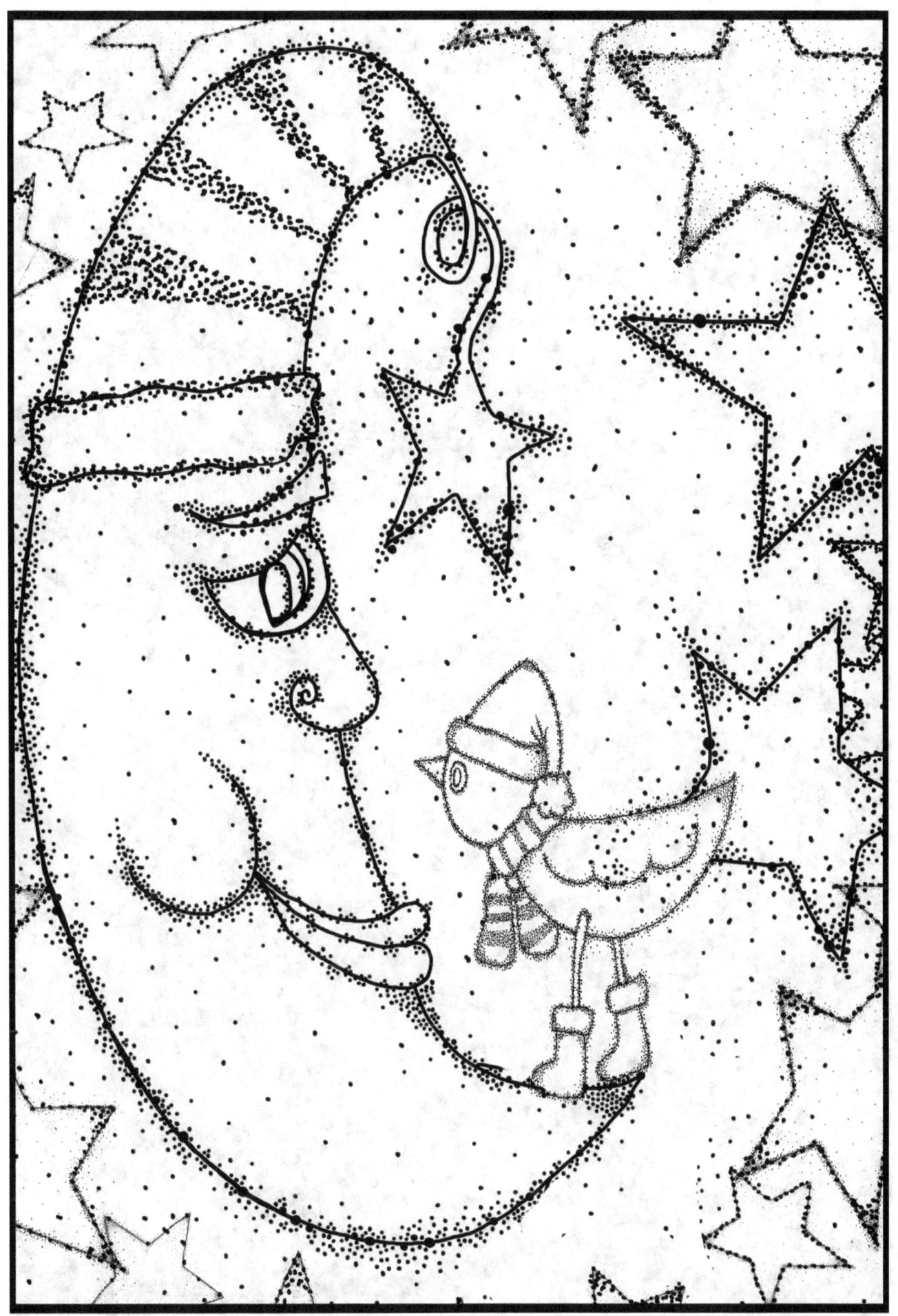

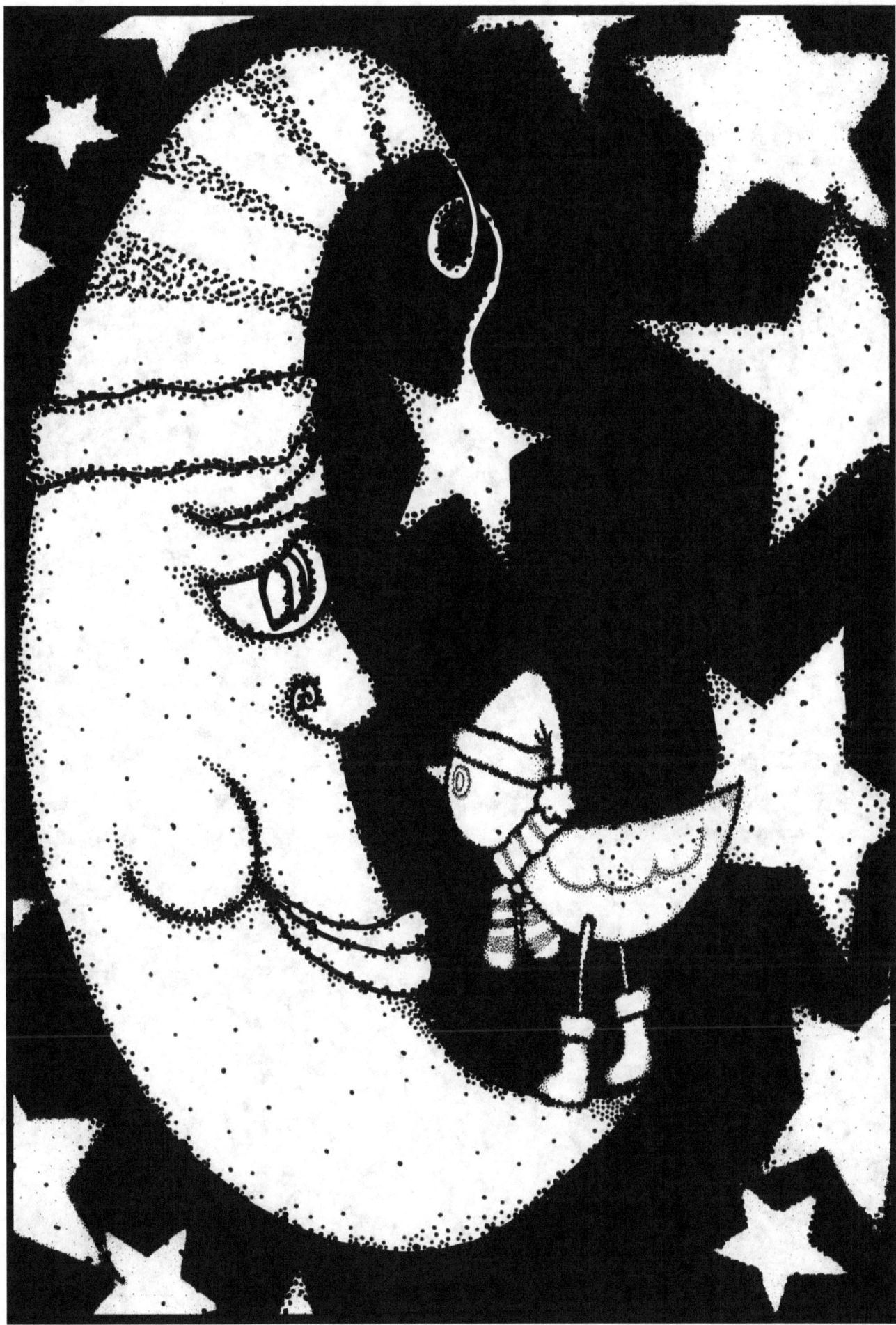

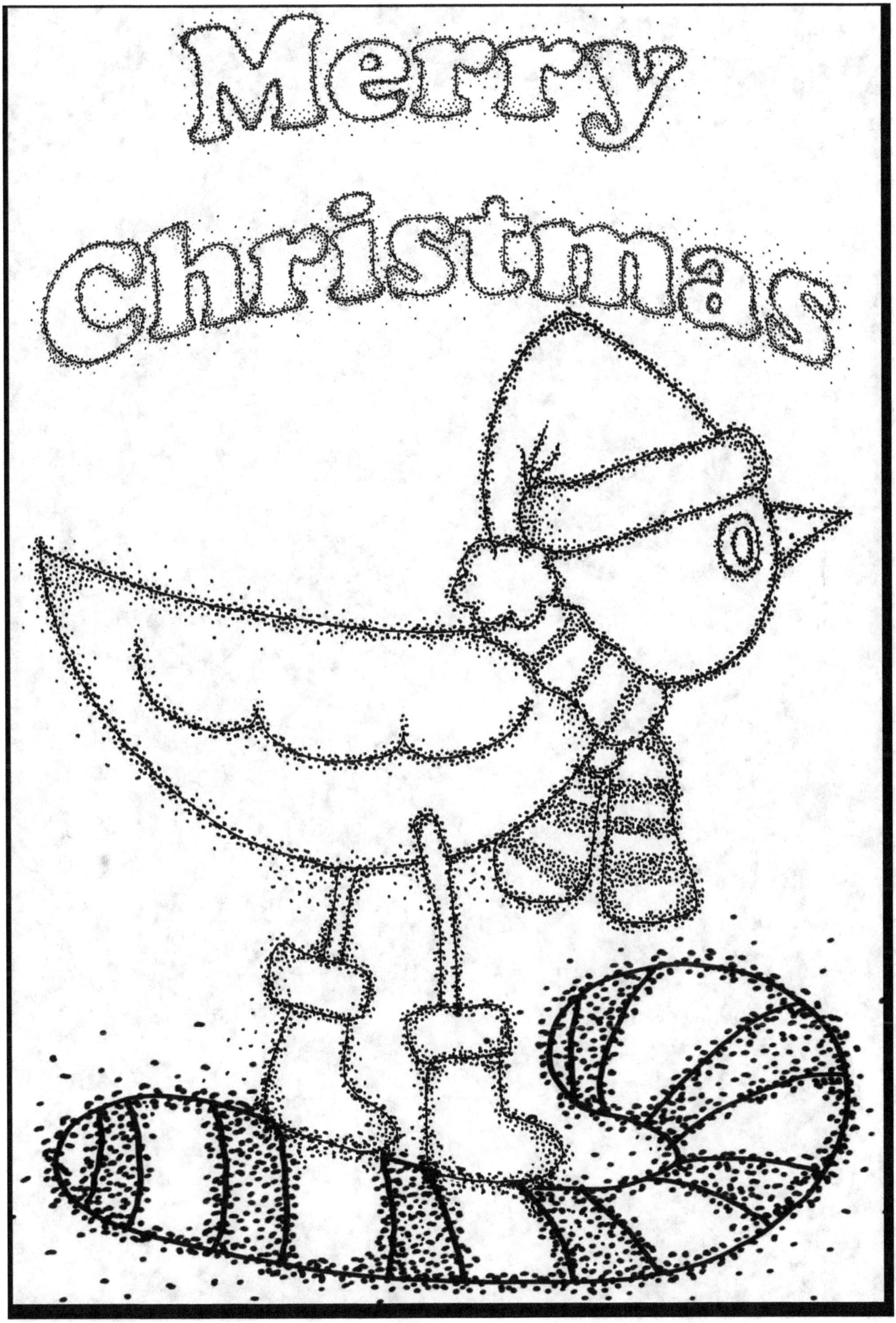
Merry
Christmas

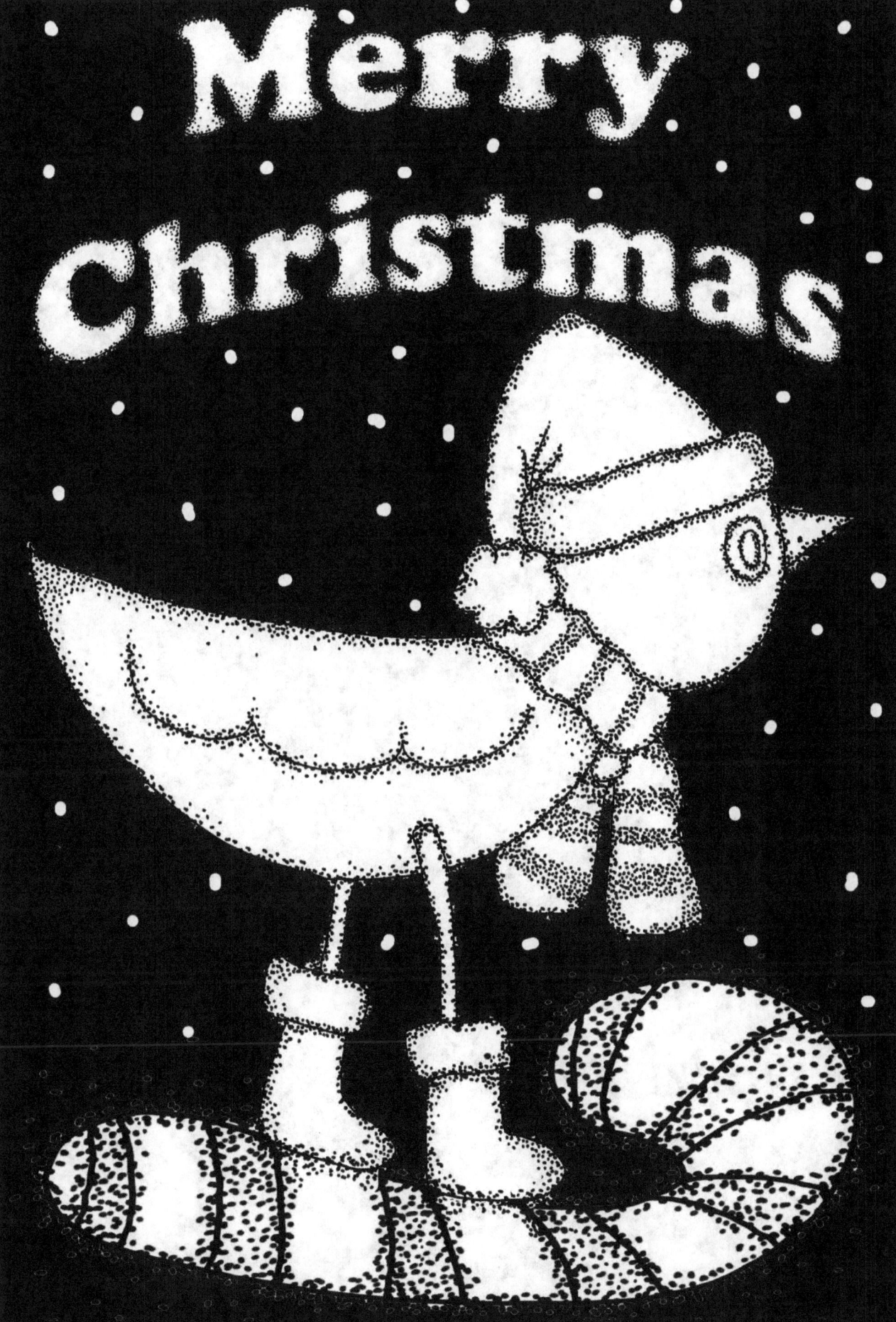

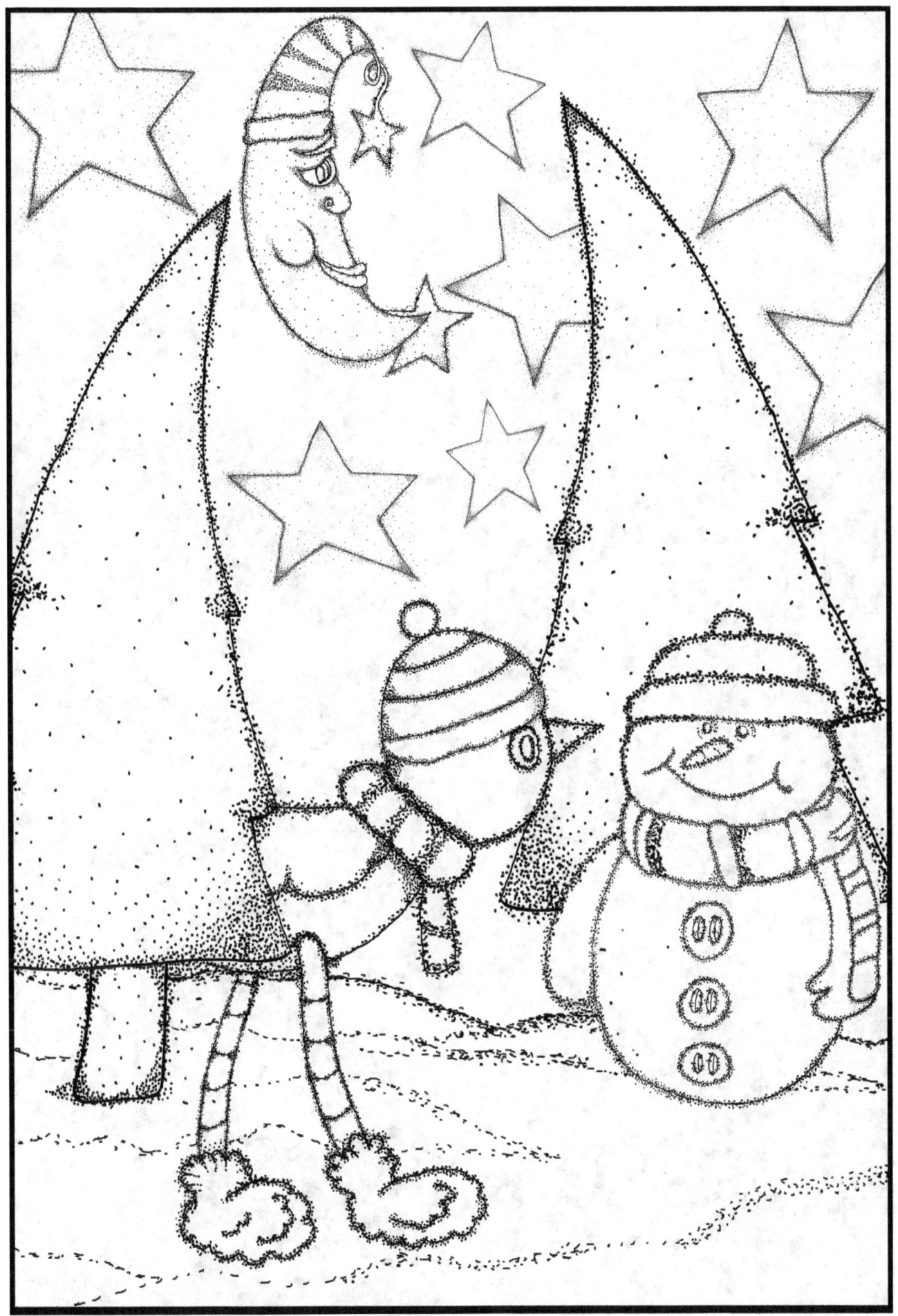

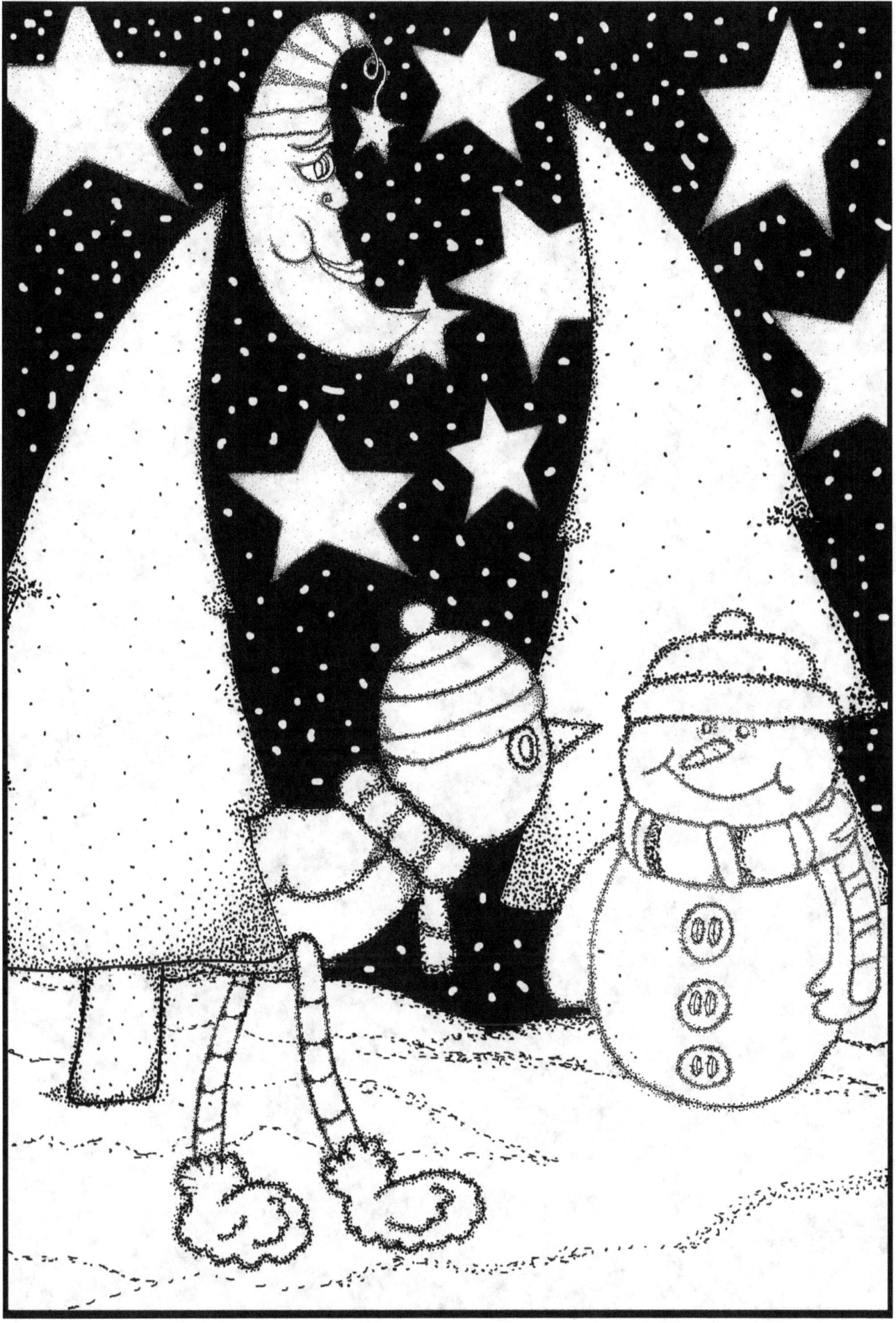

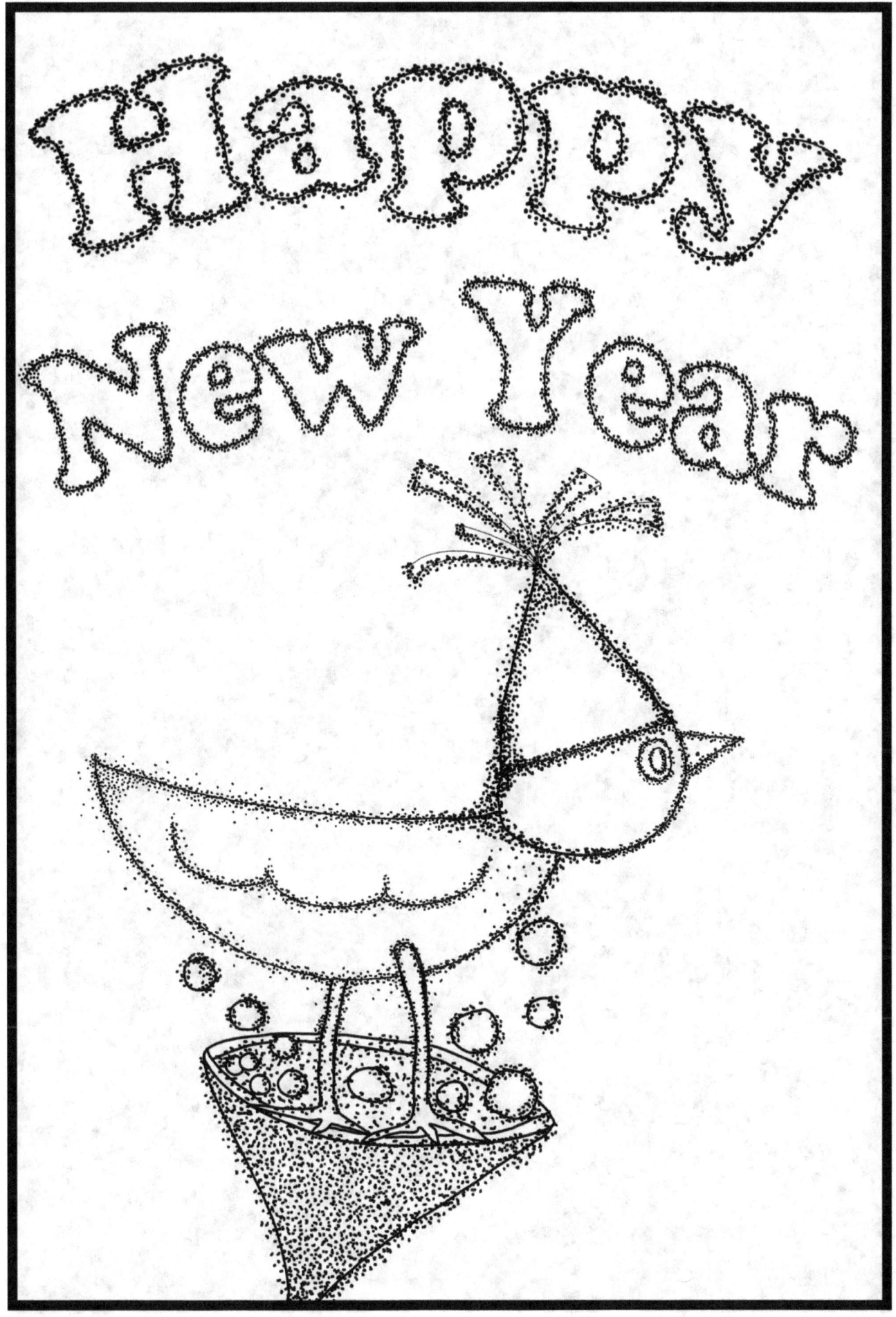

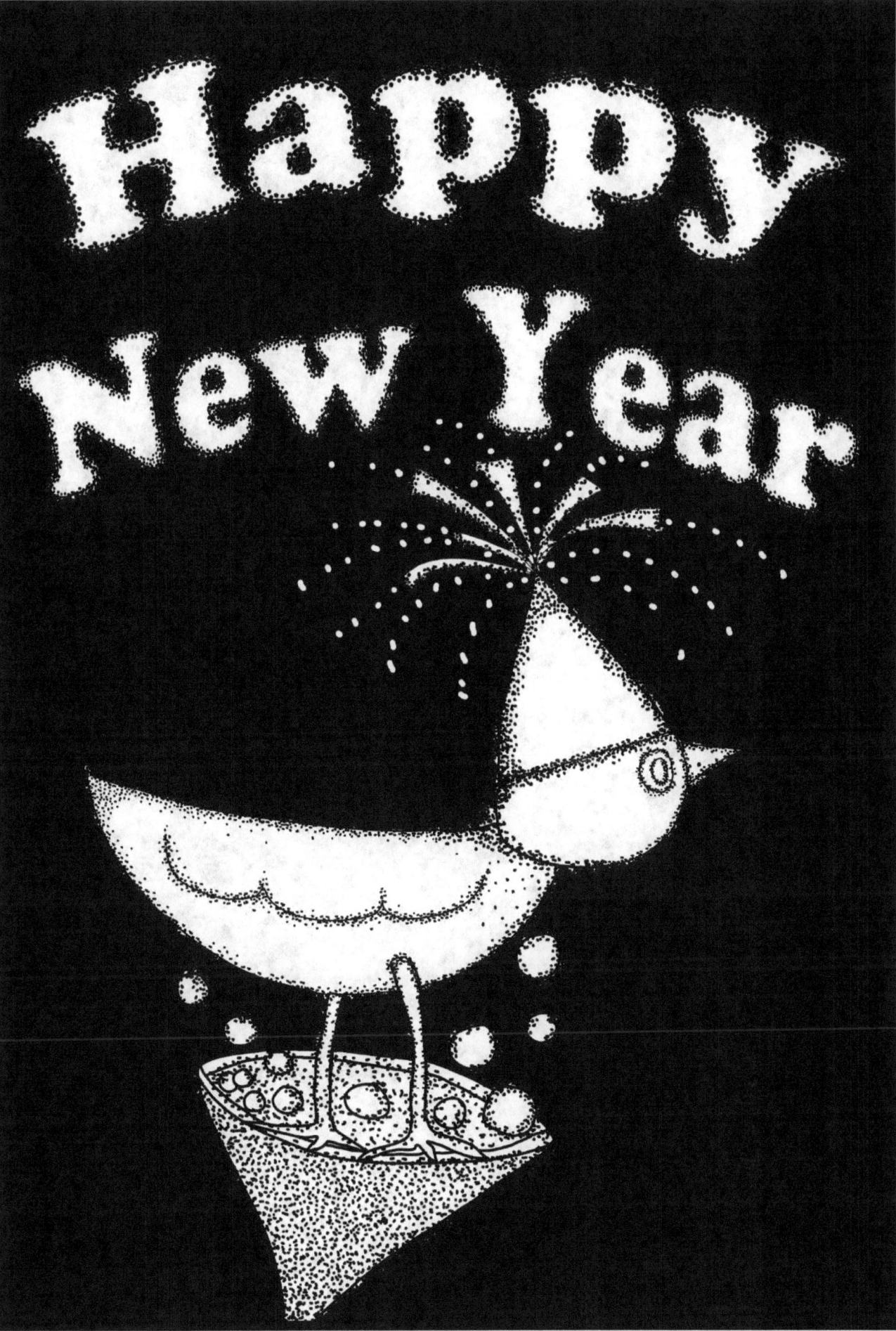

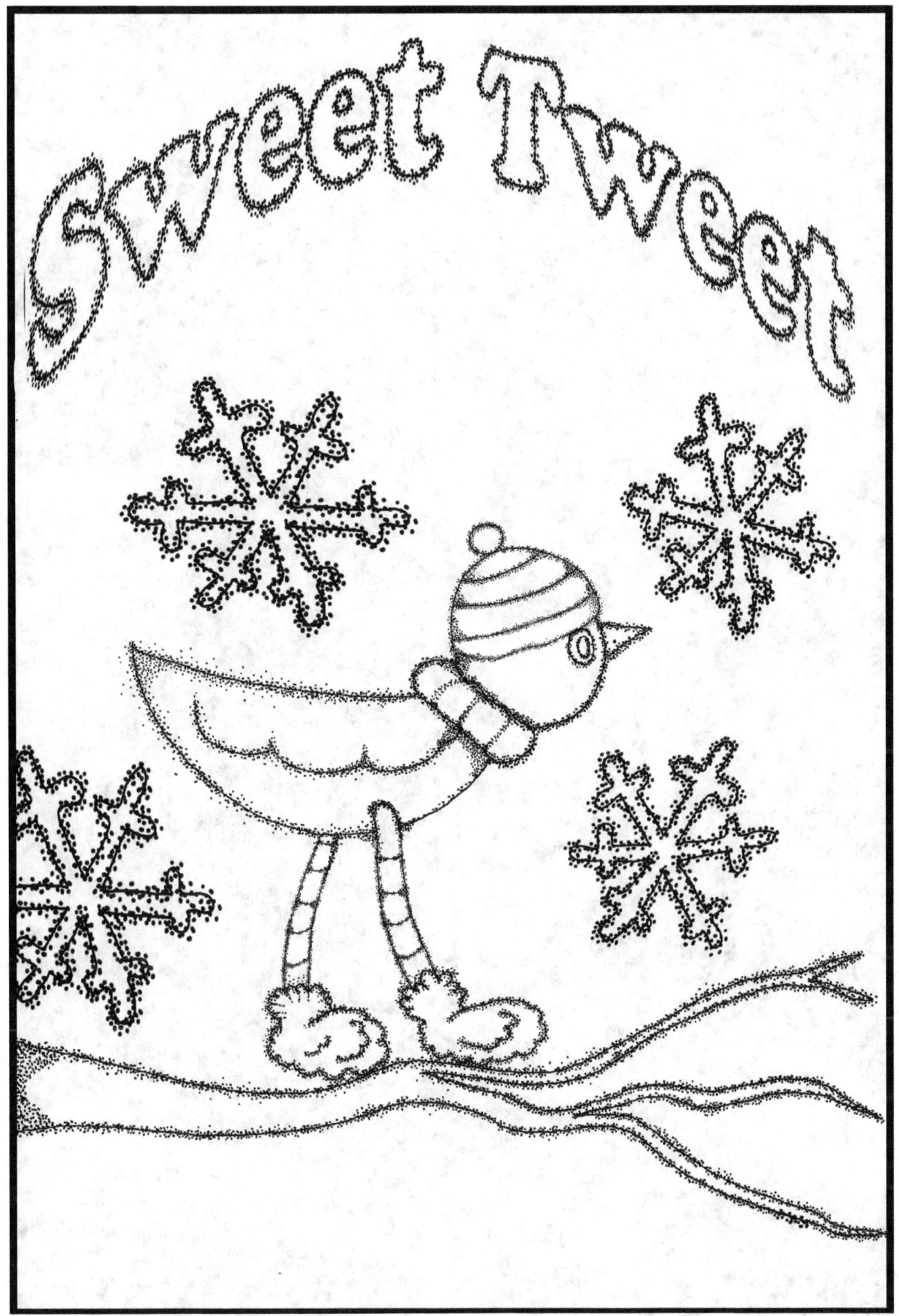

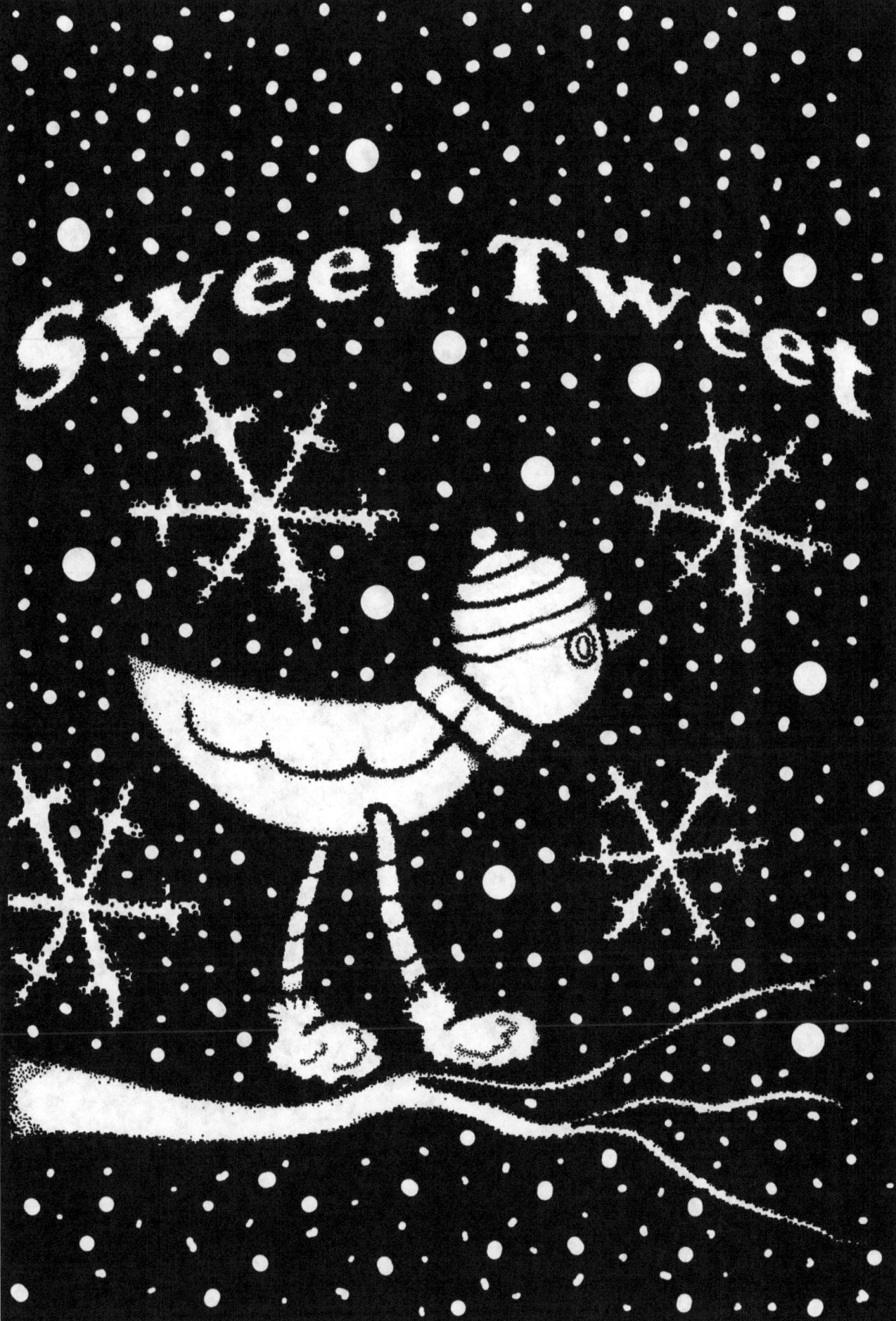

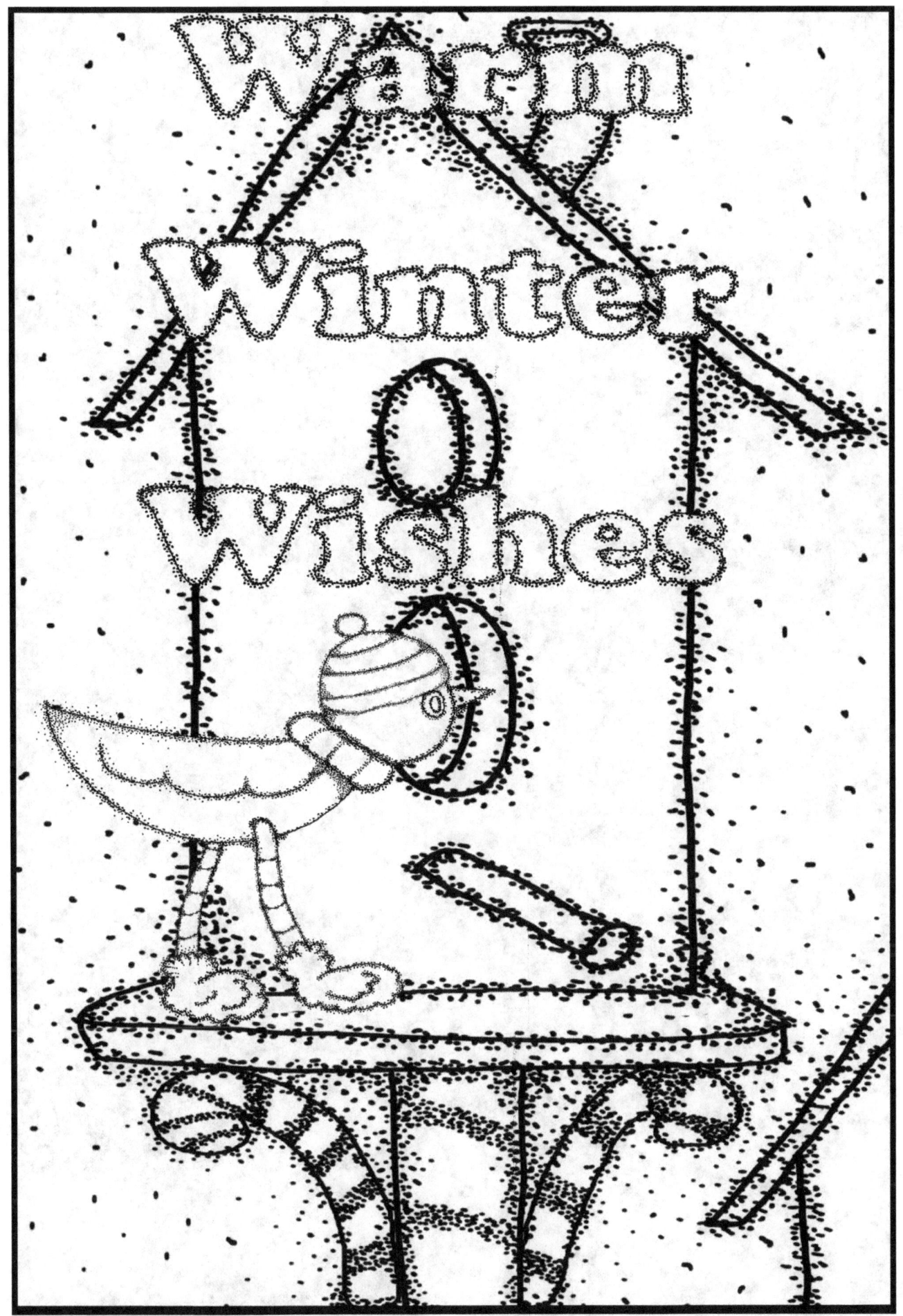

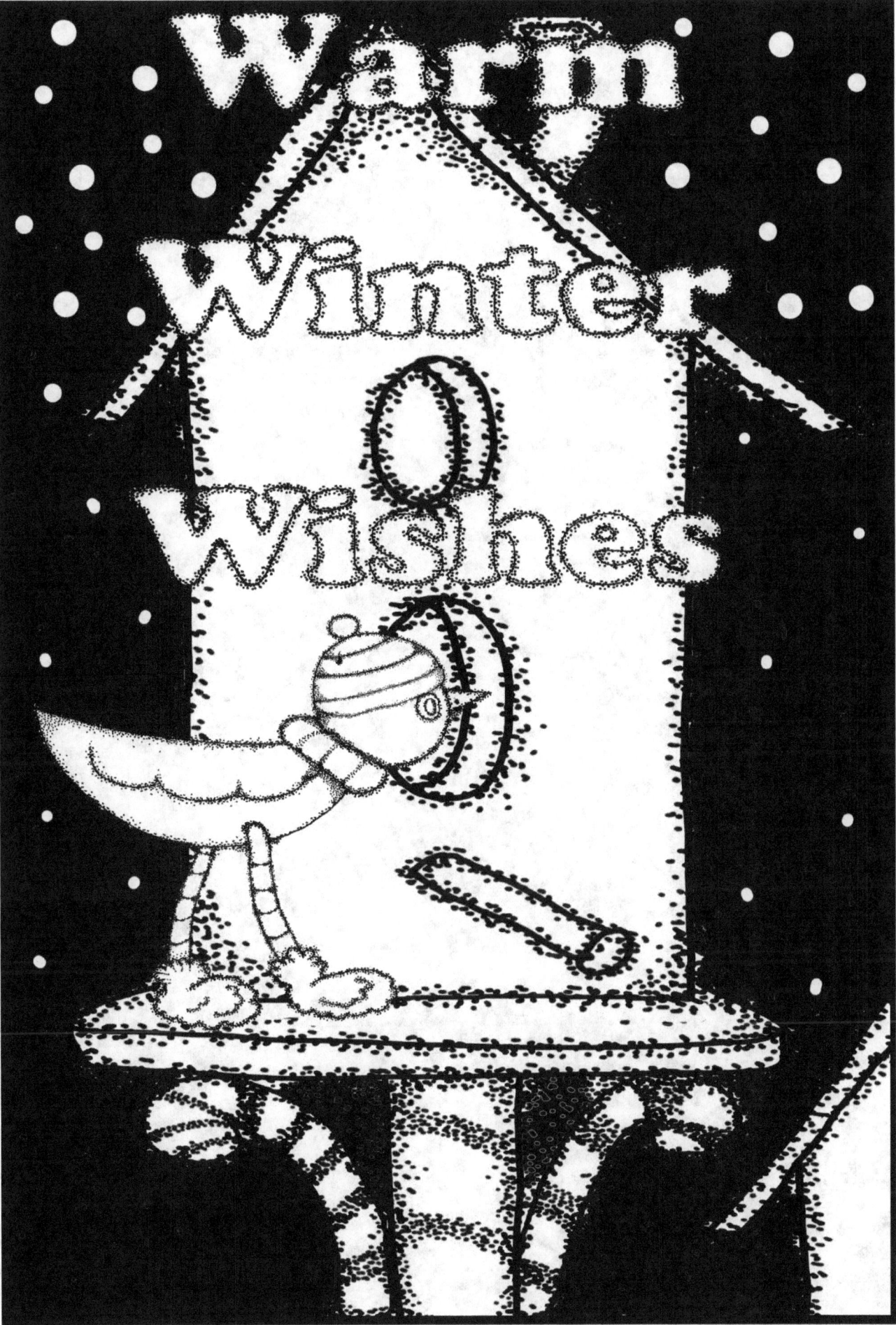

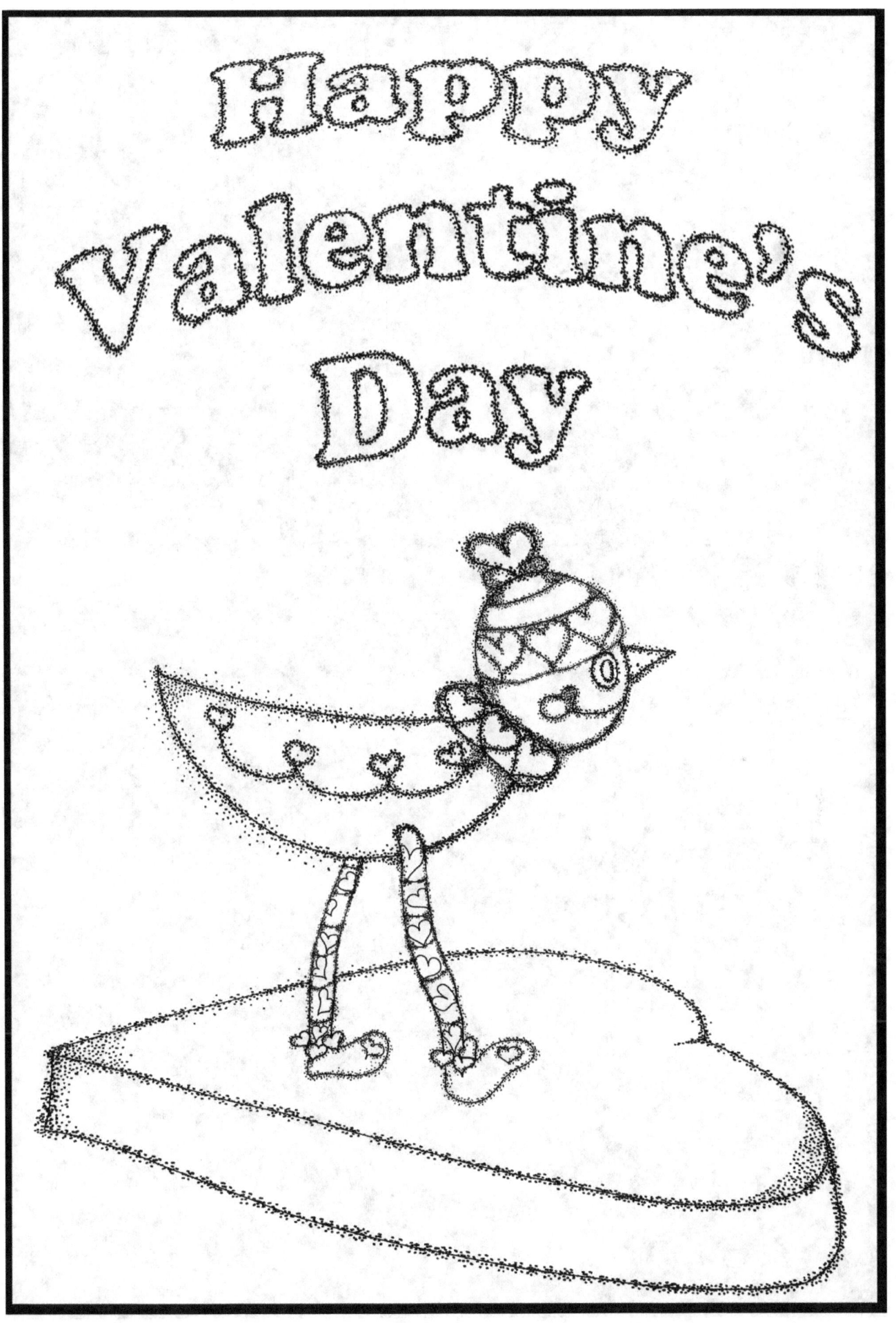

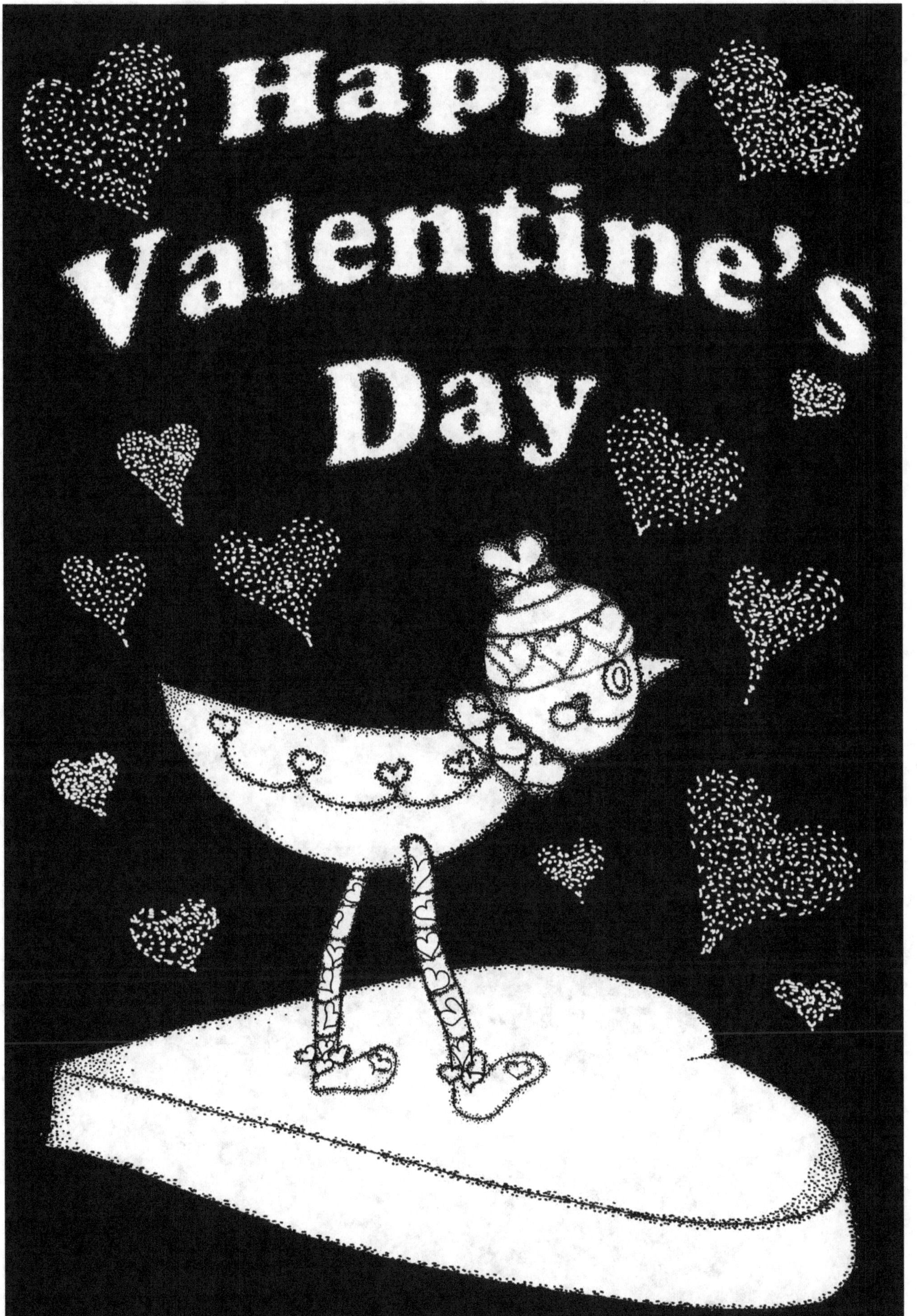
Happy
Valentine's
Day

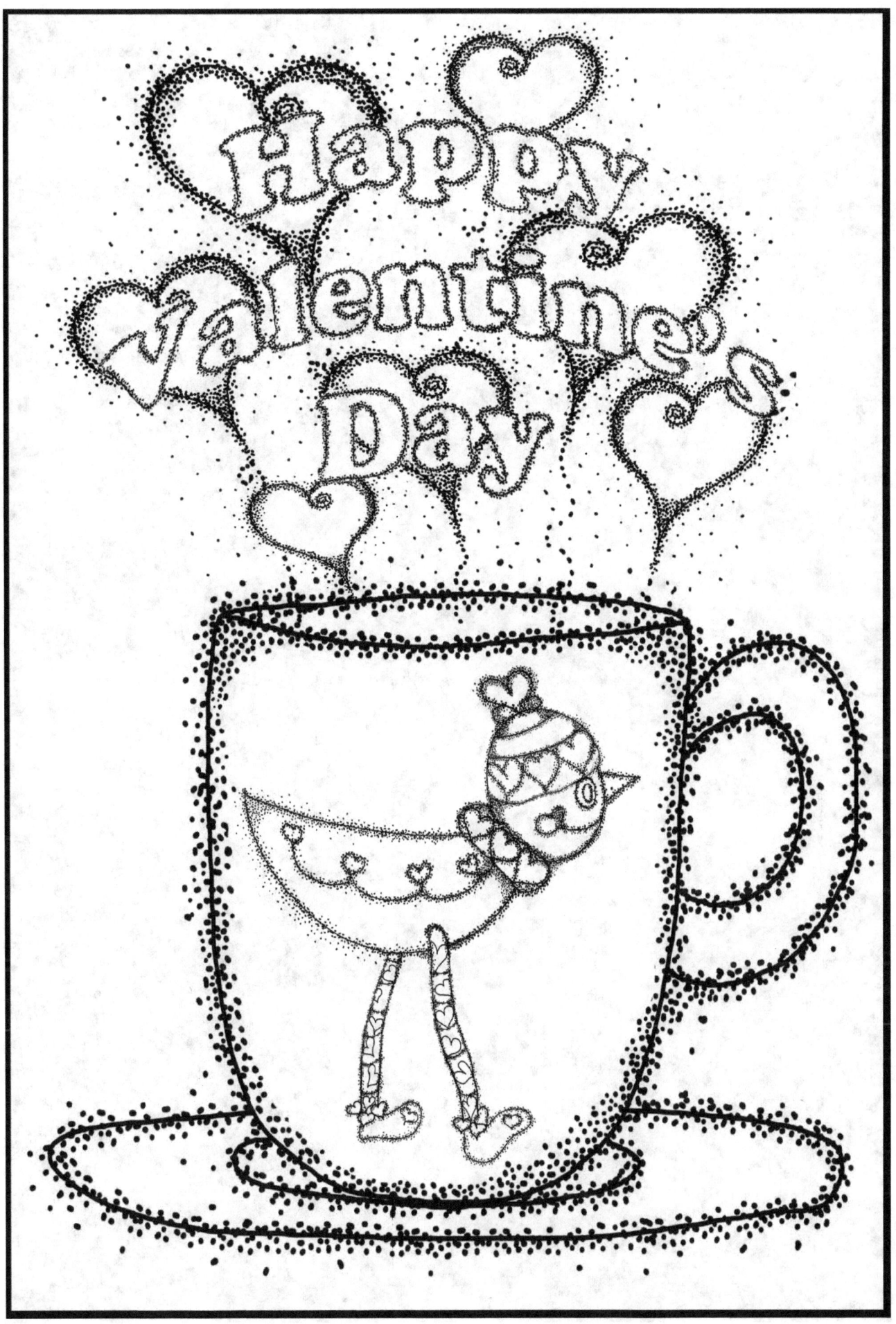

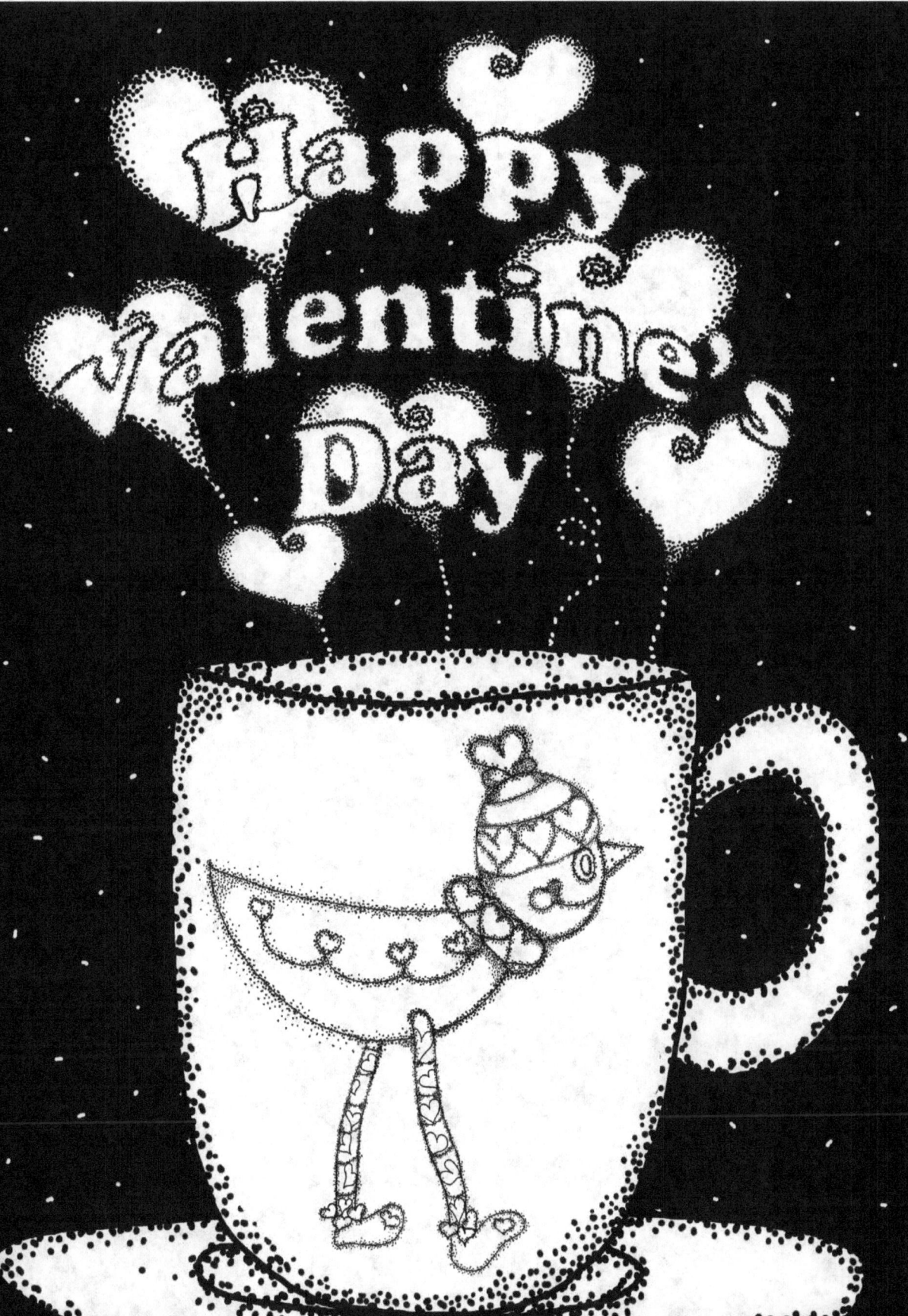

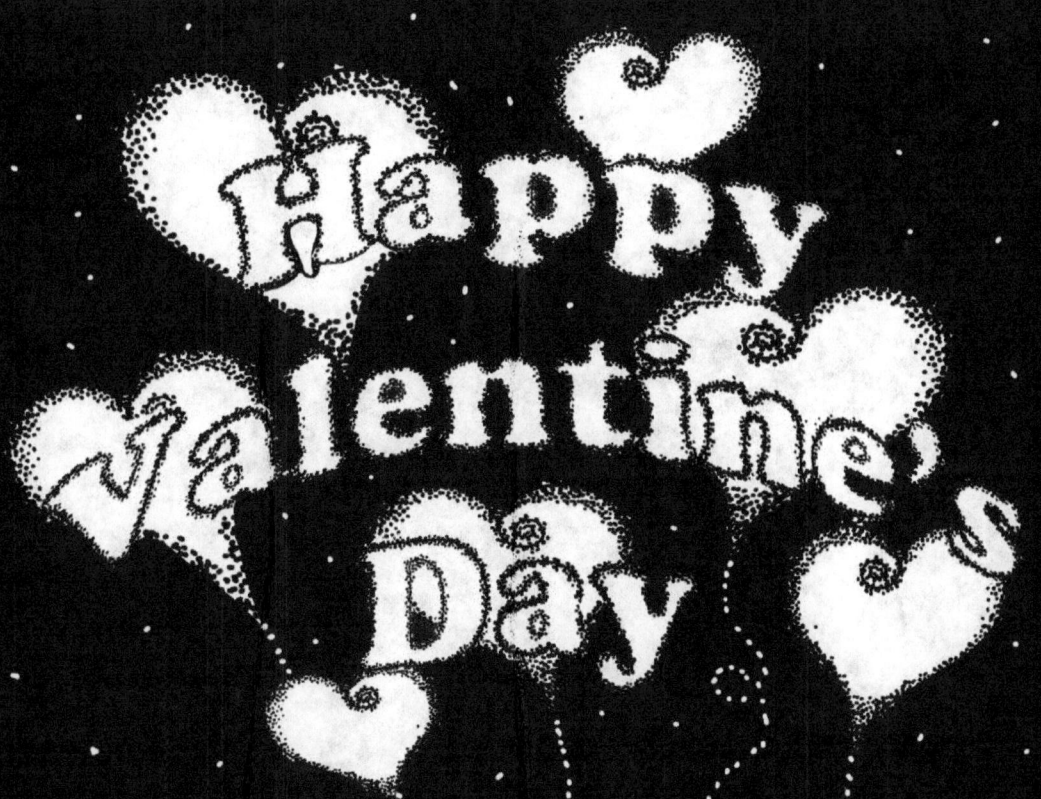
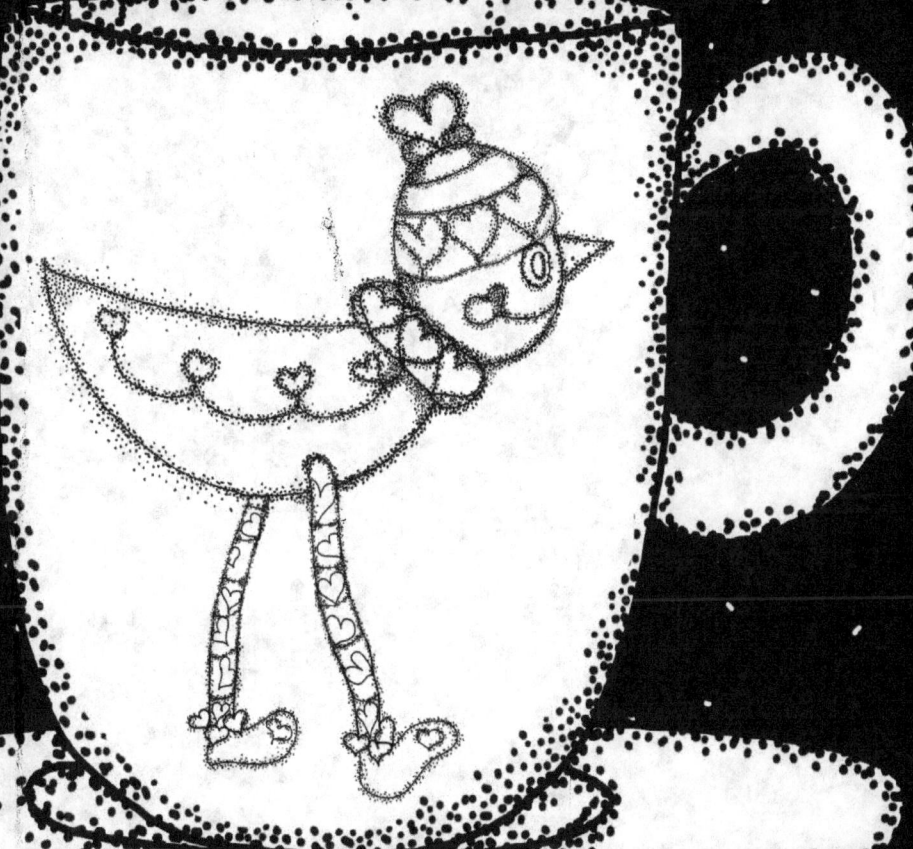

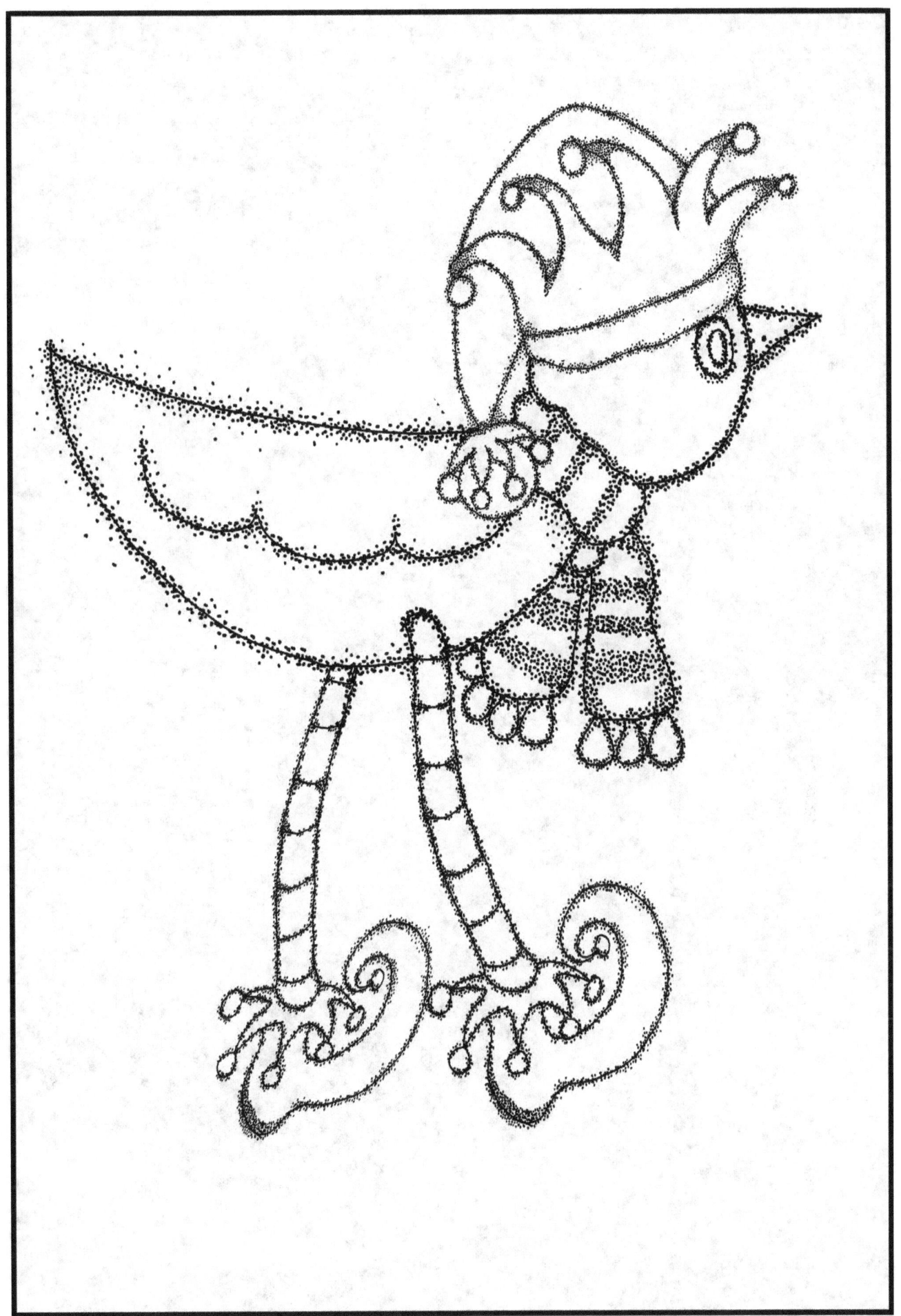

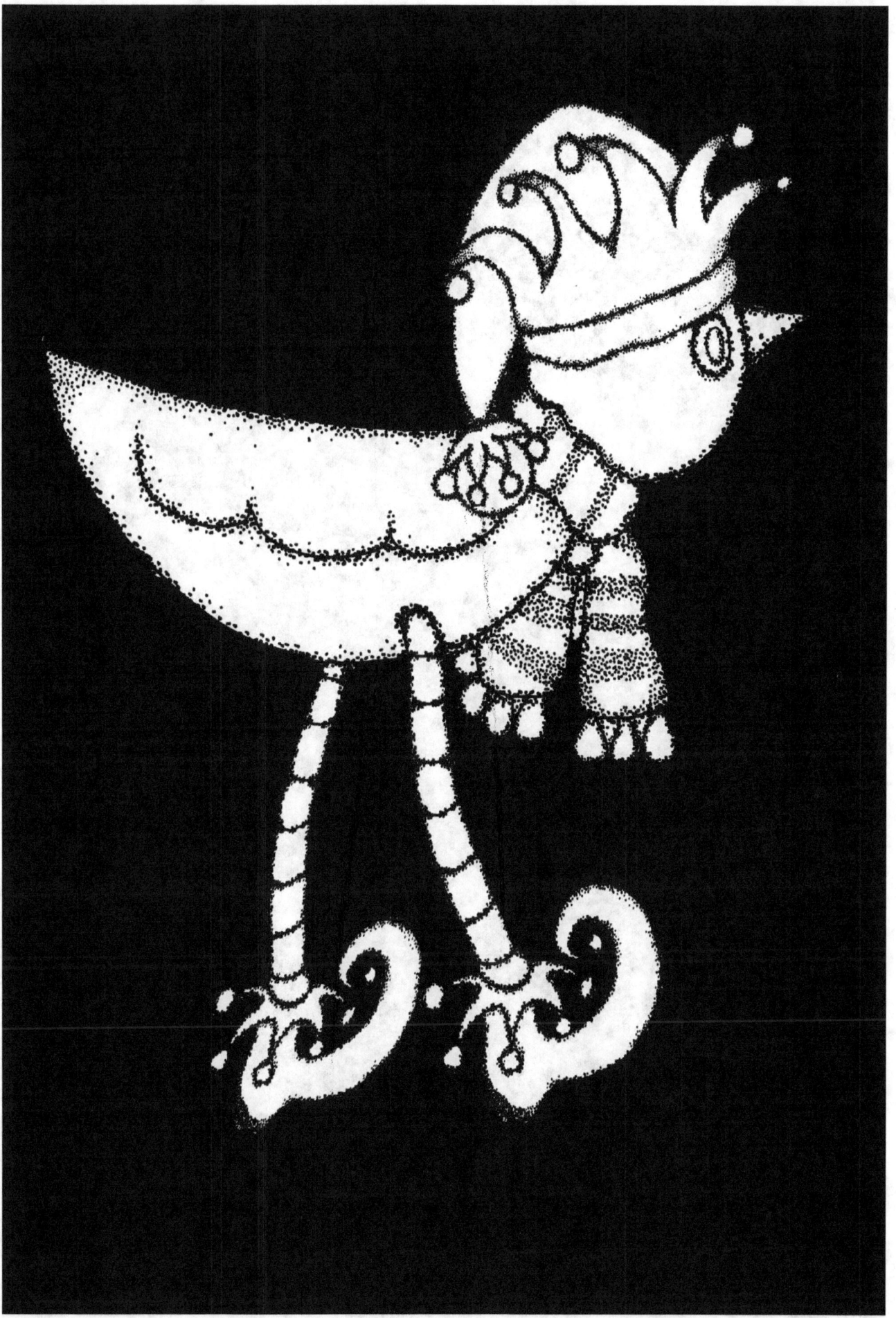

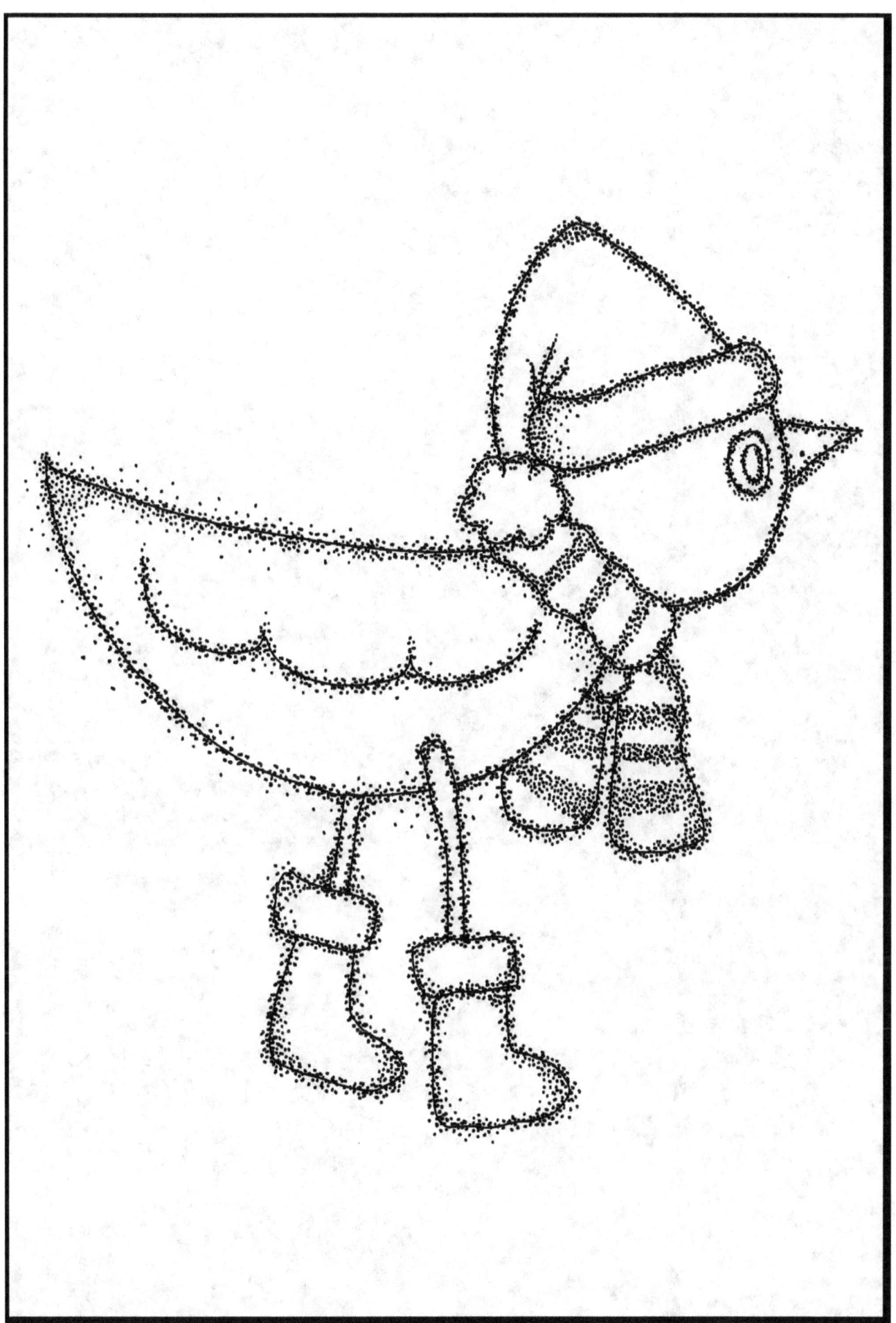

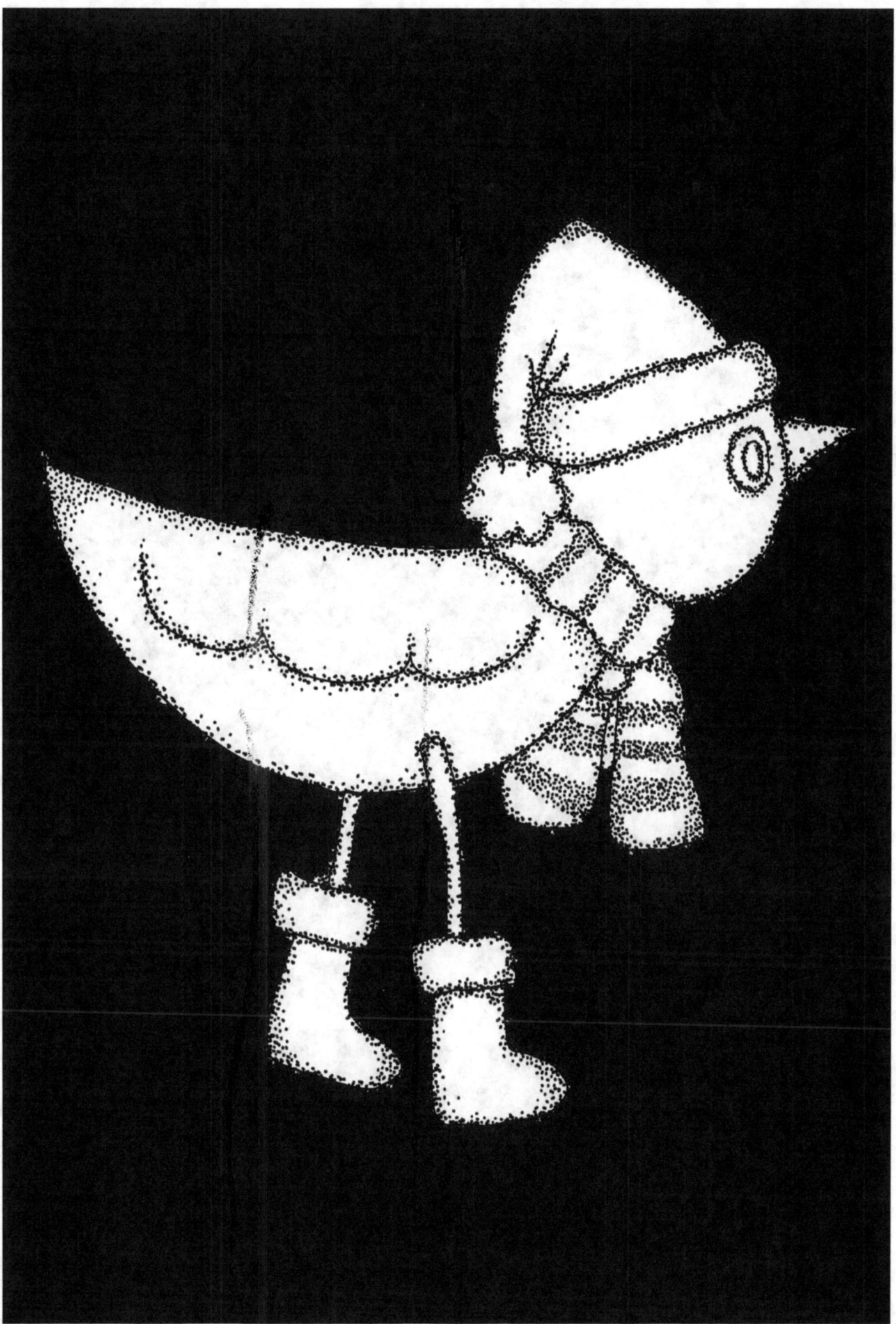

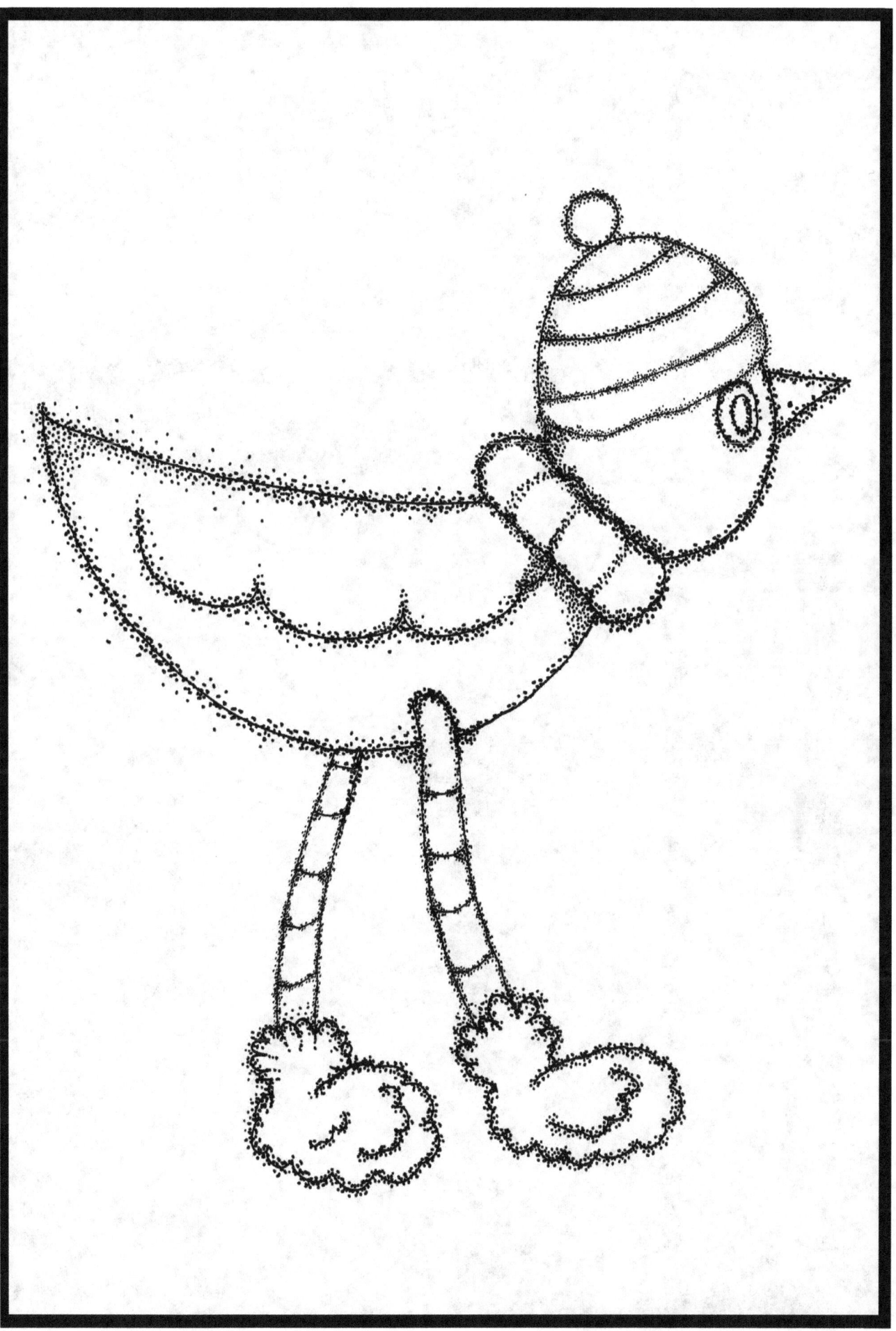

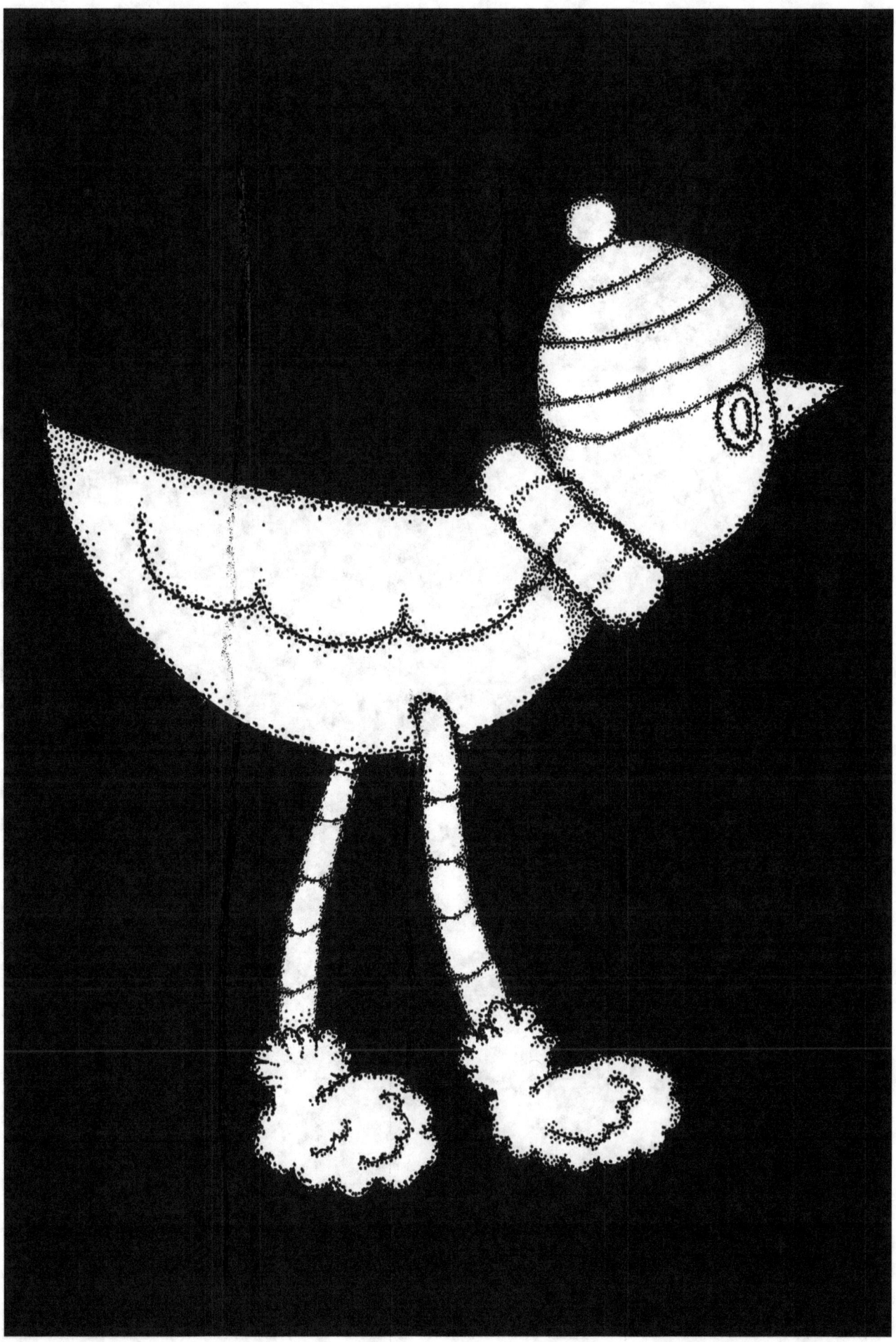

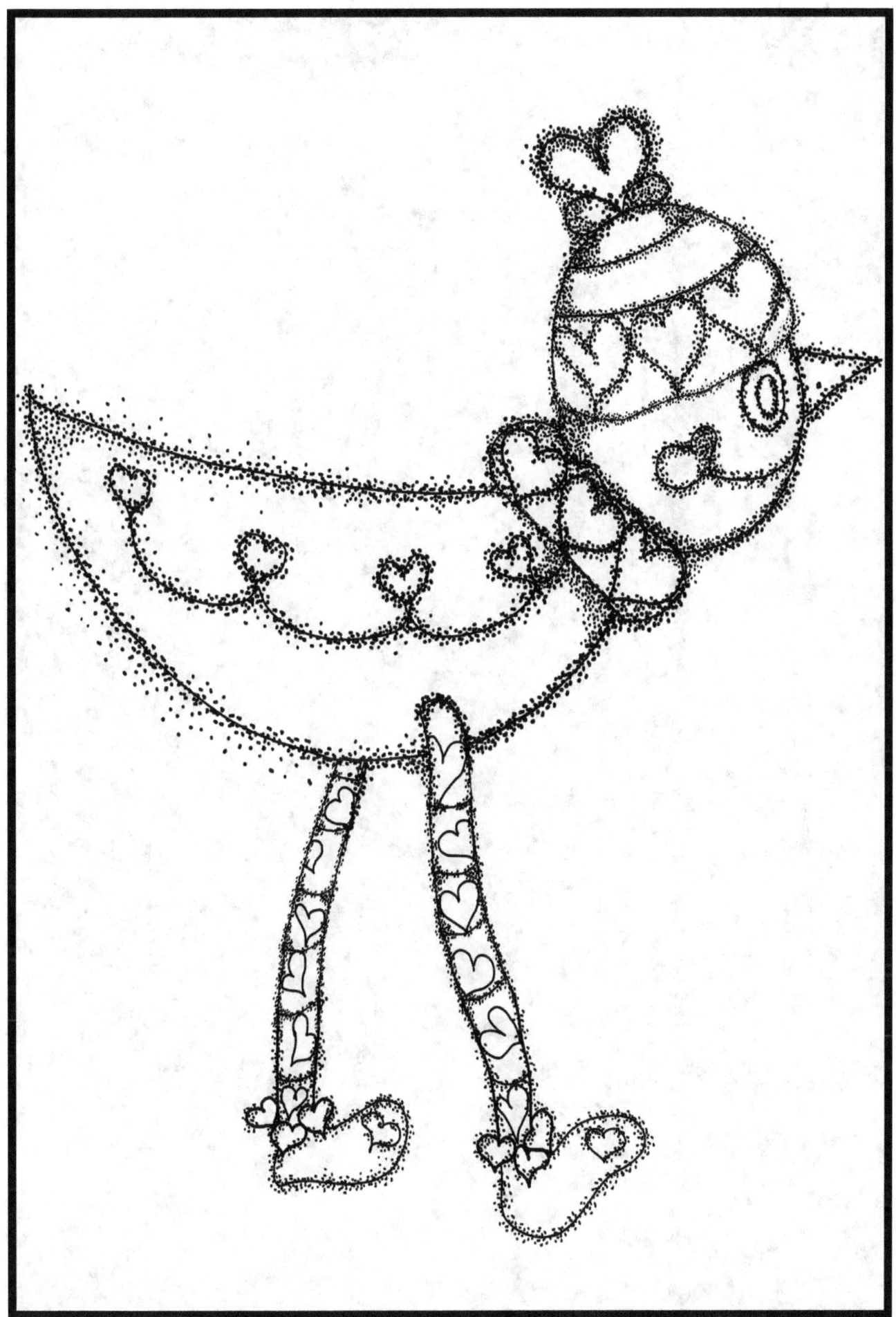

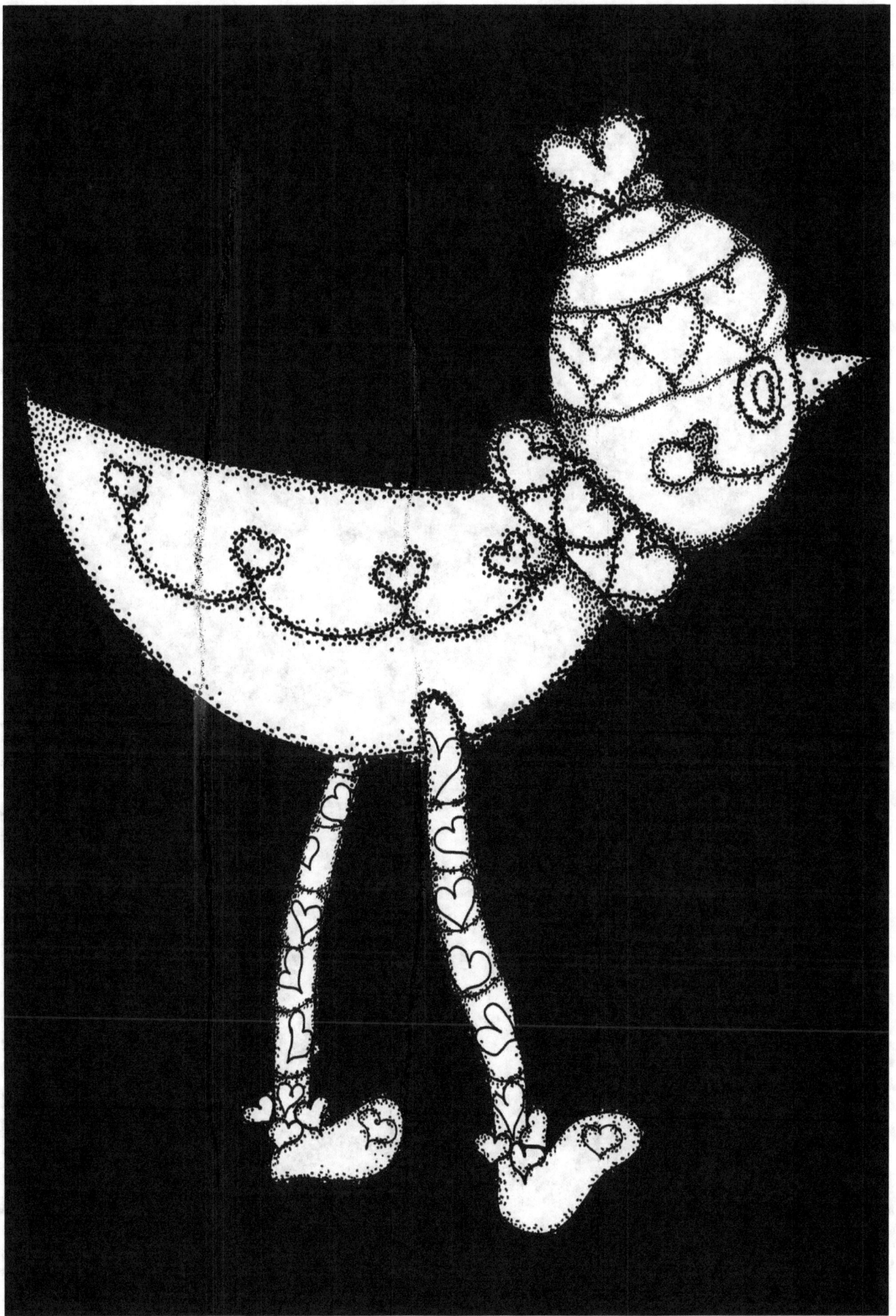

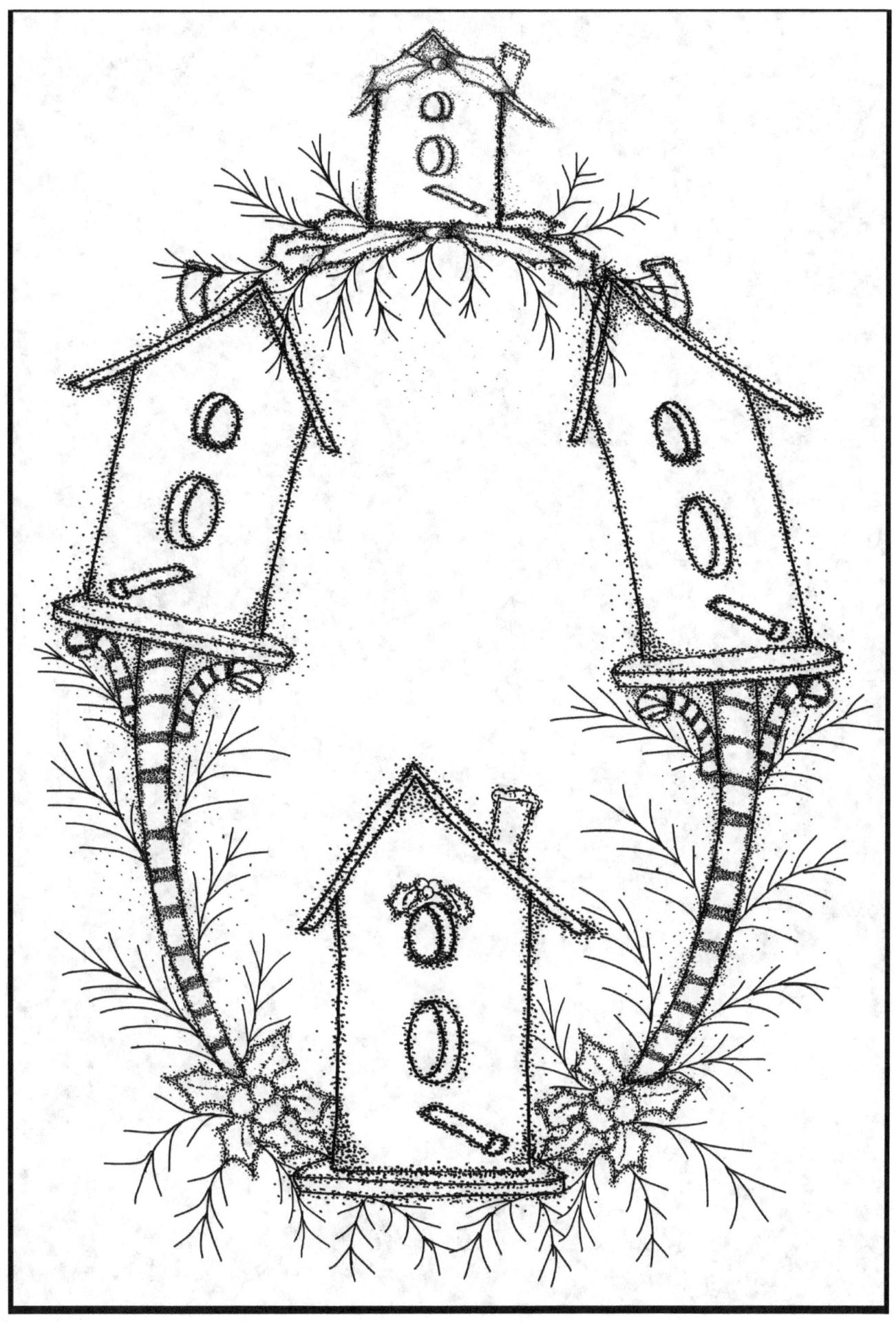

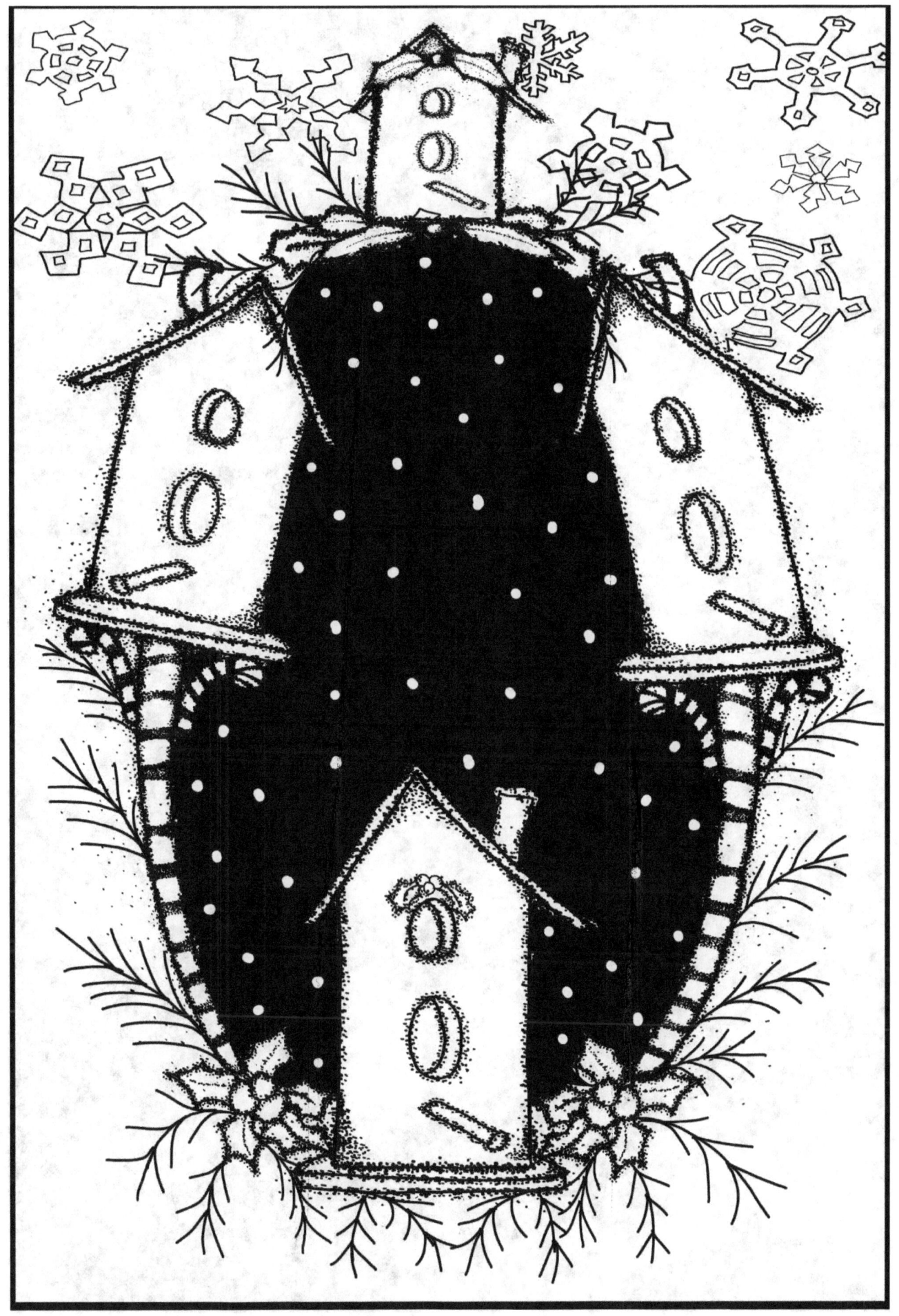

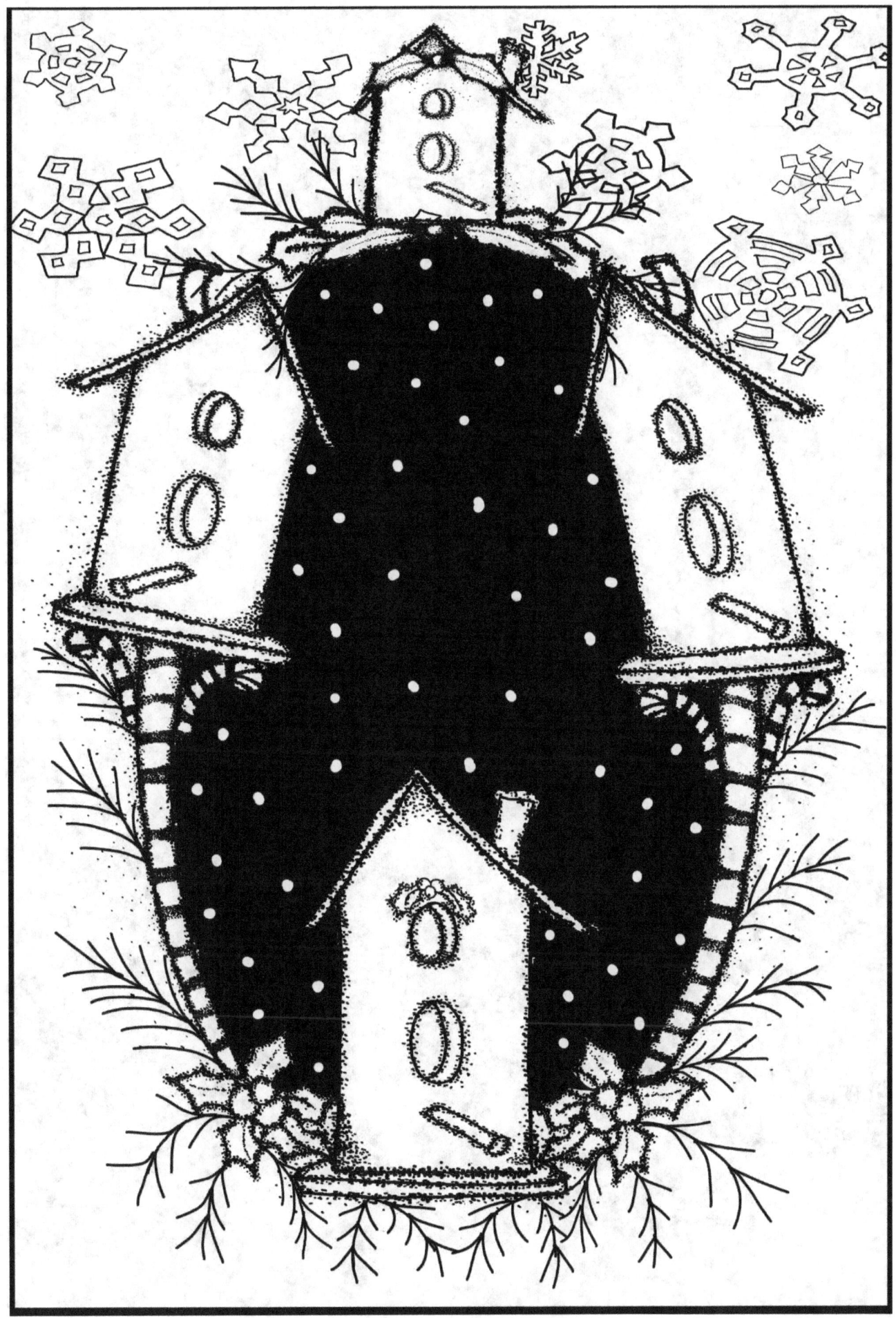

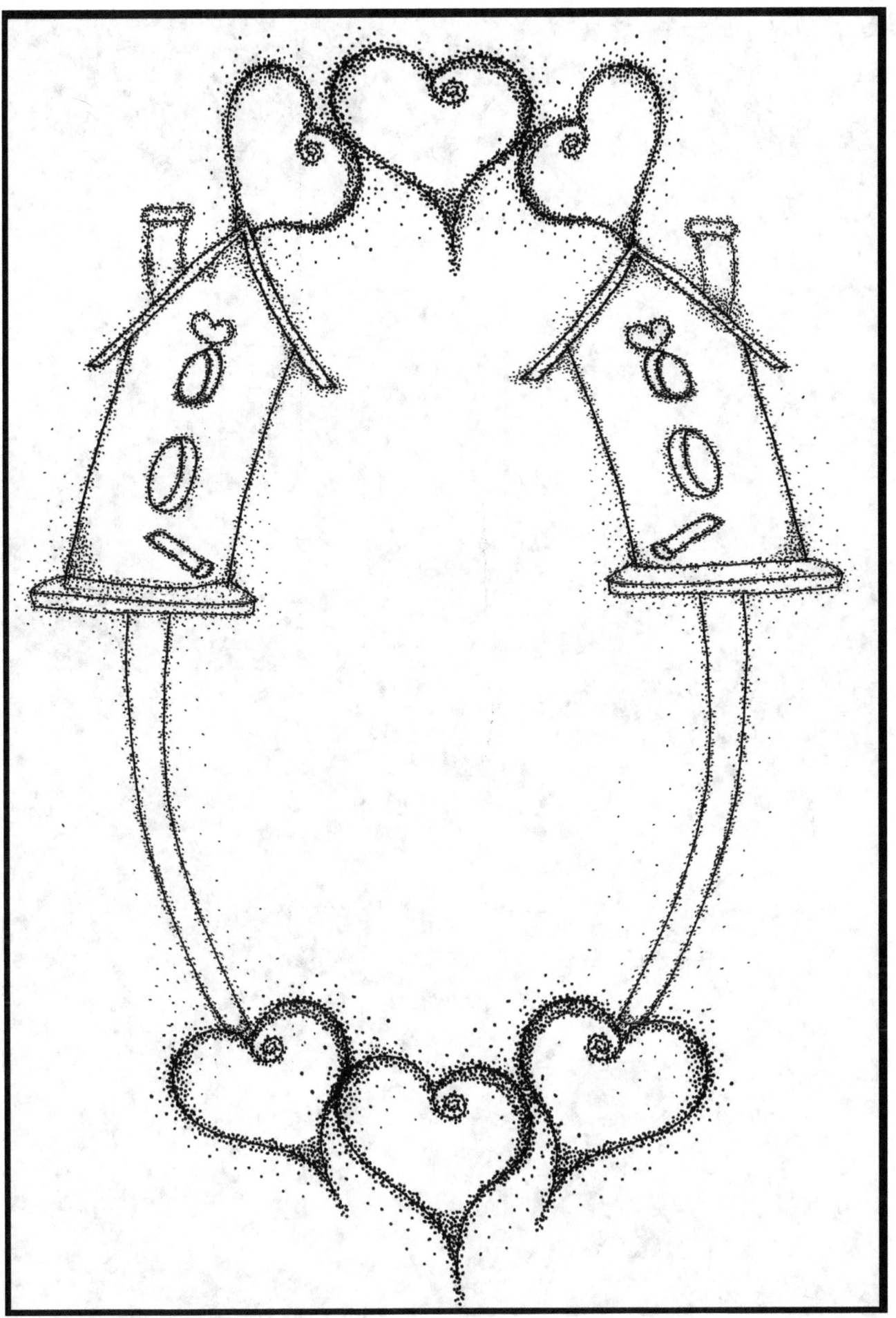

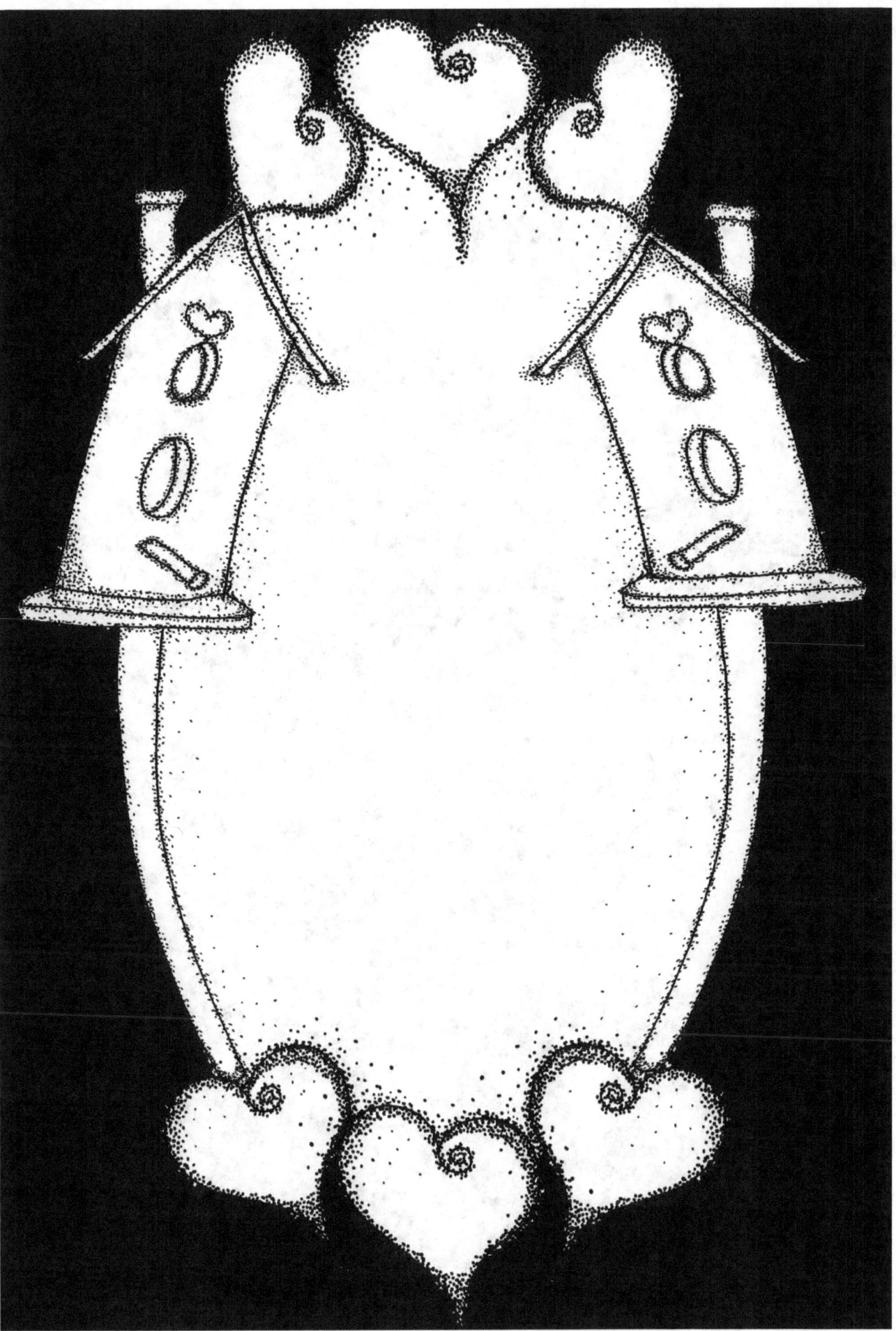

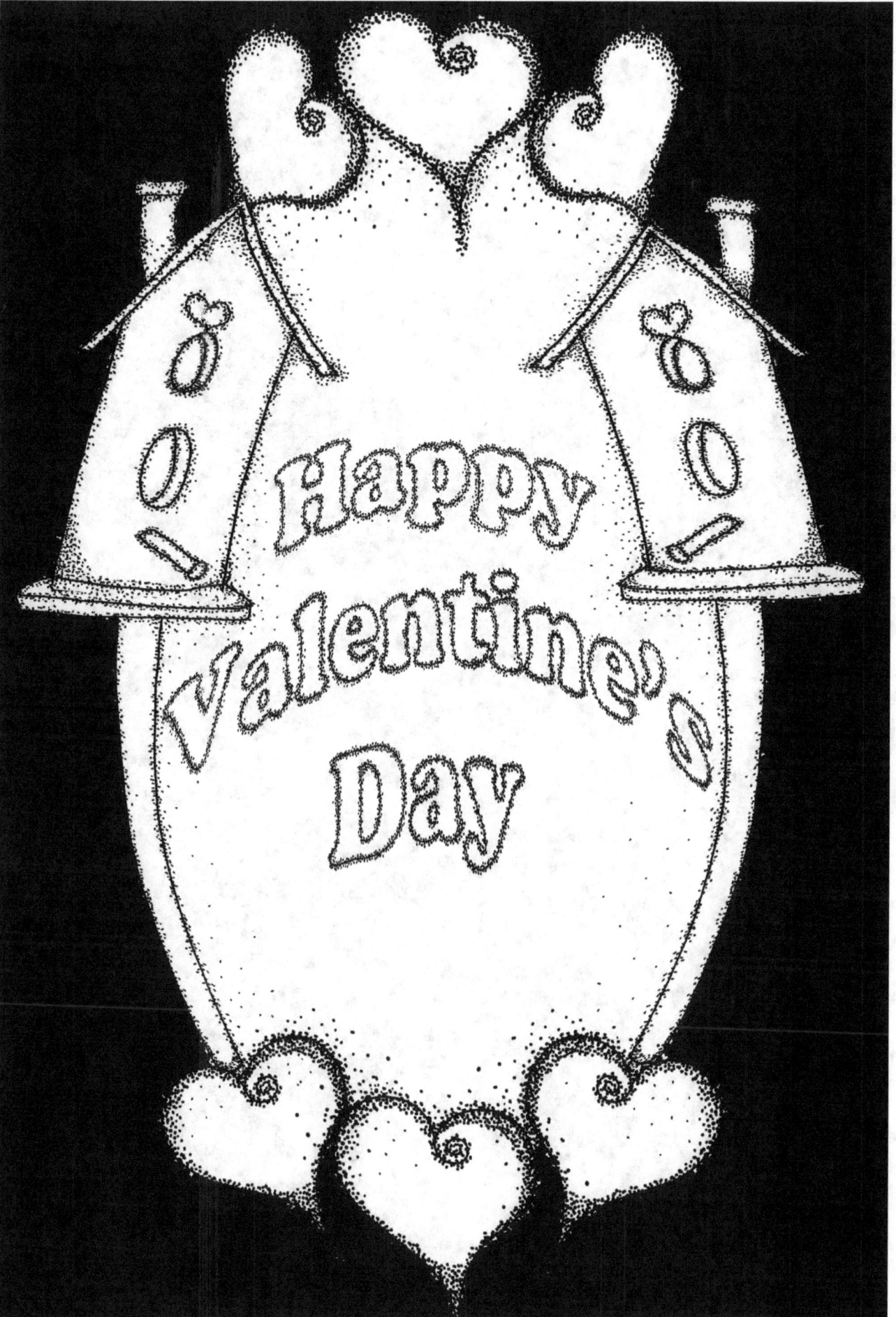

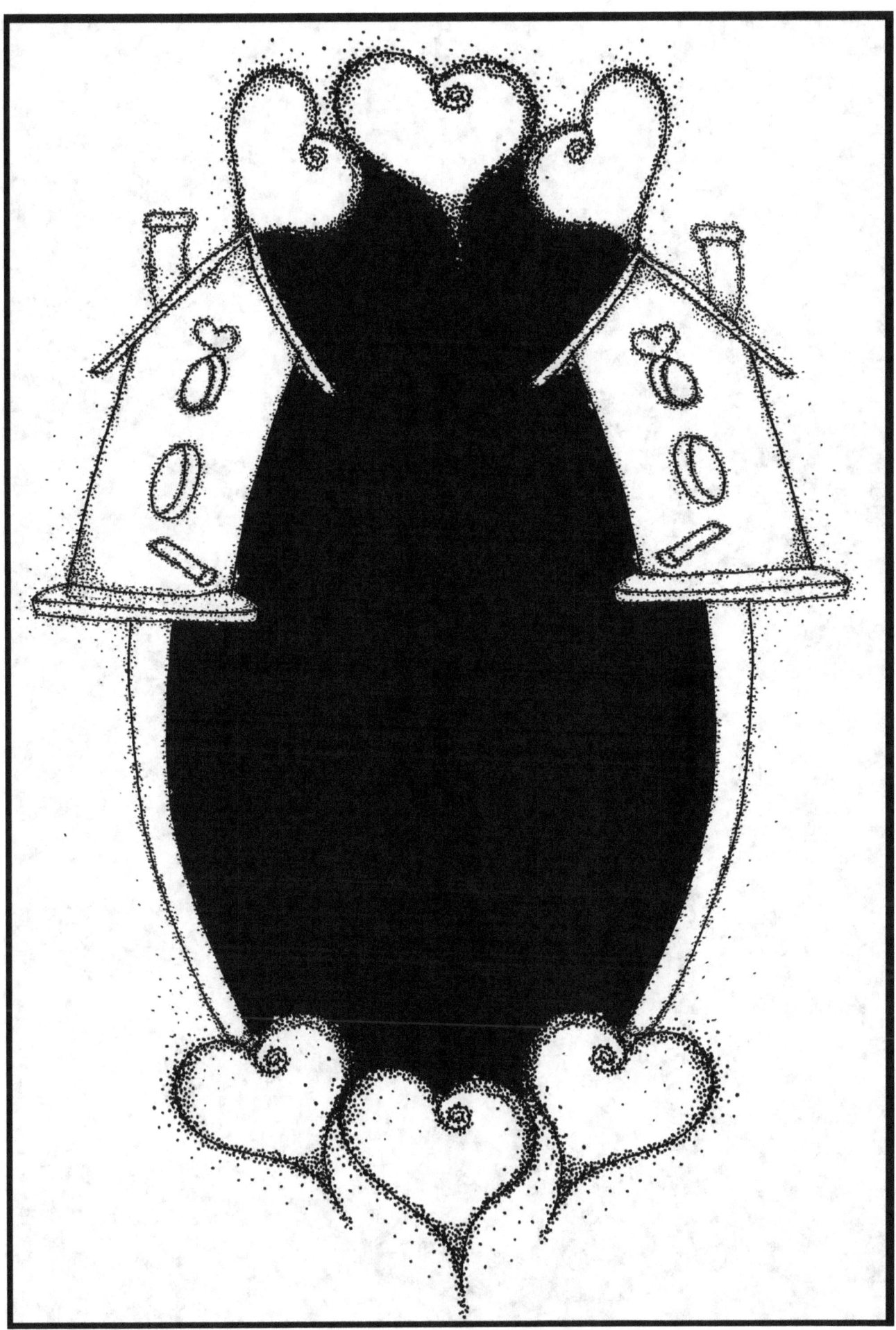

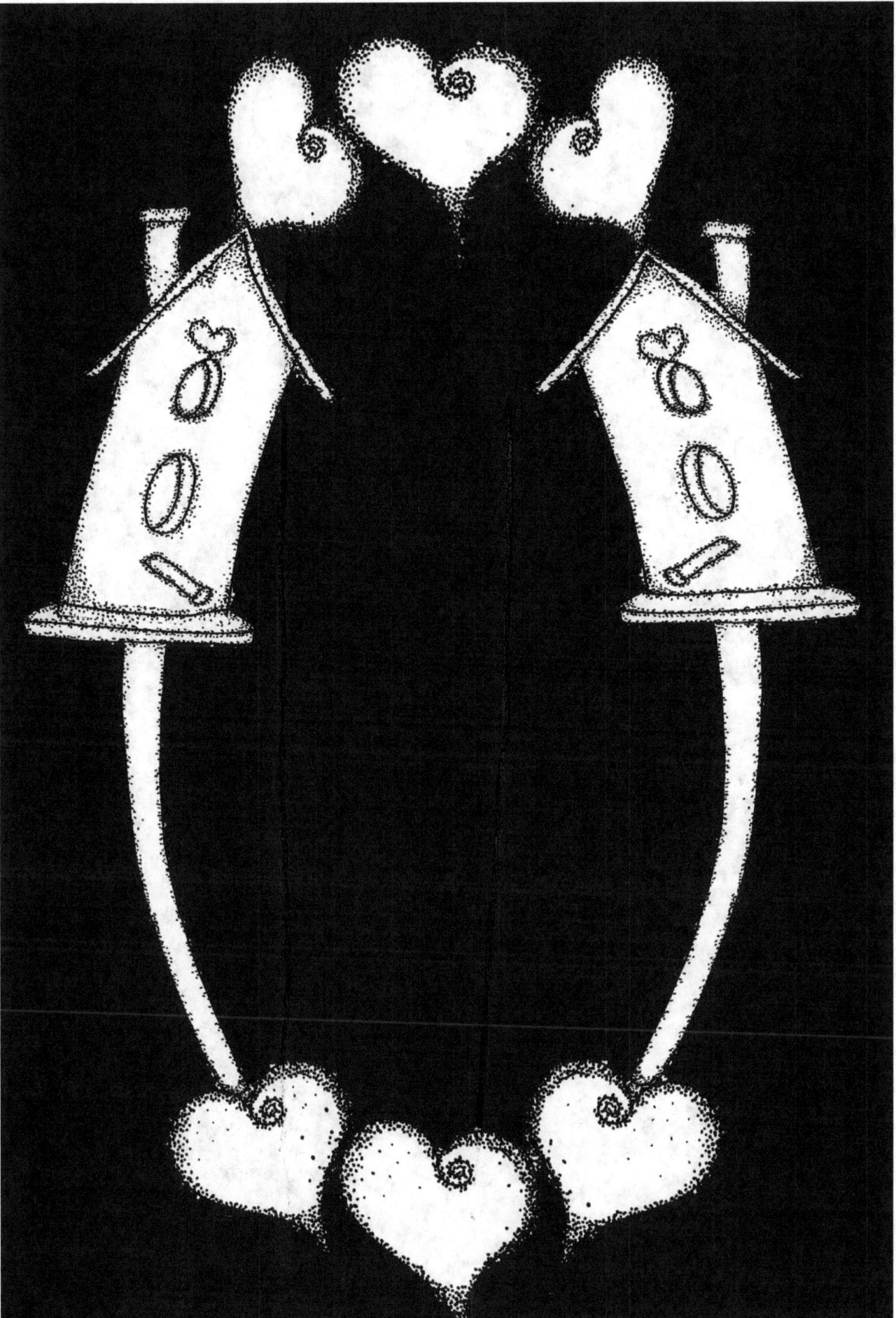

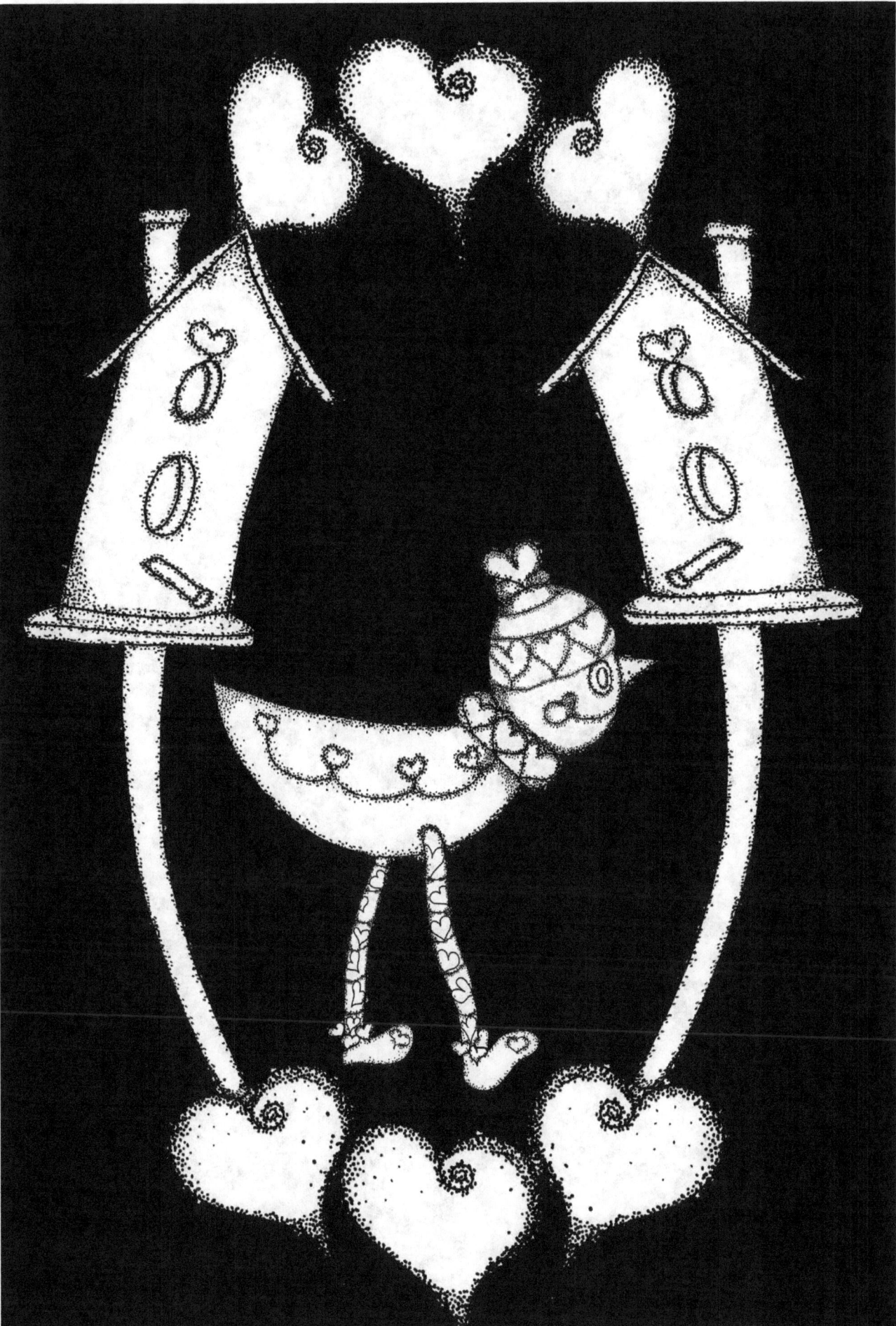

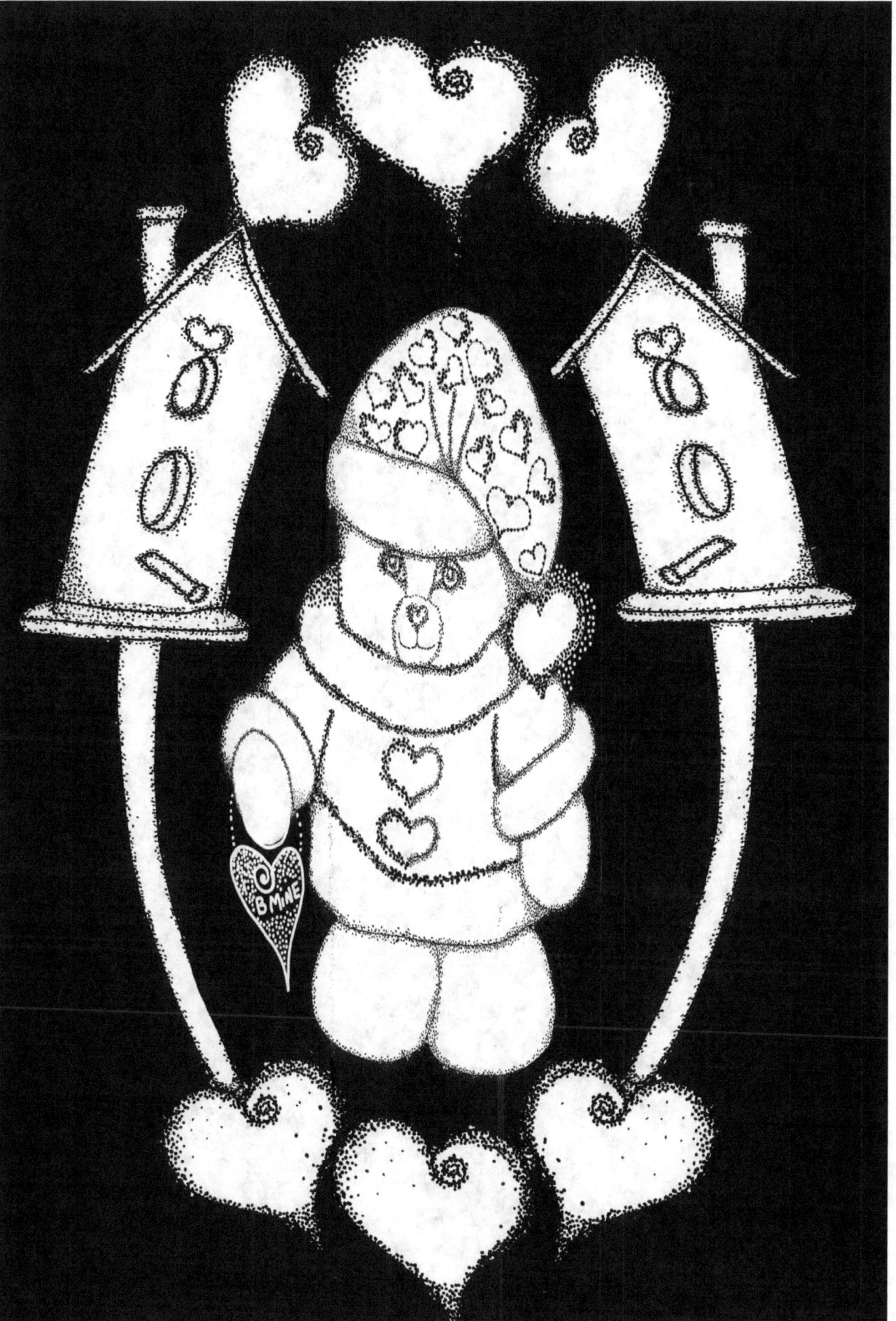

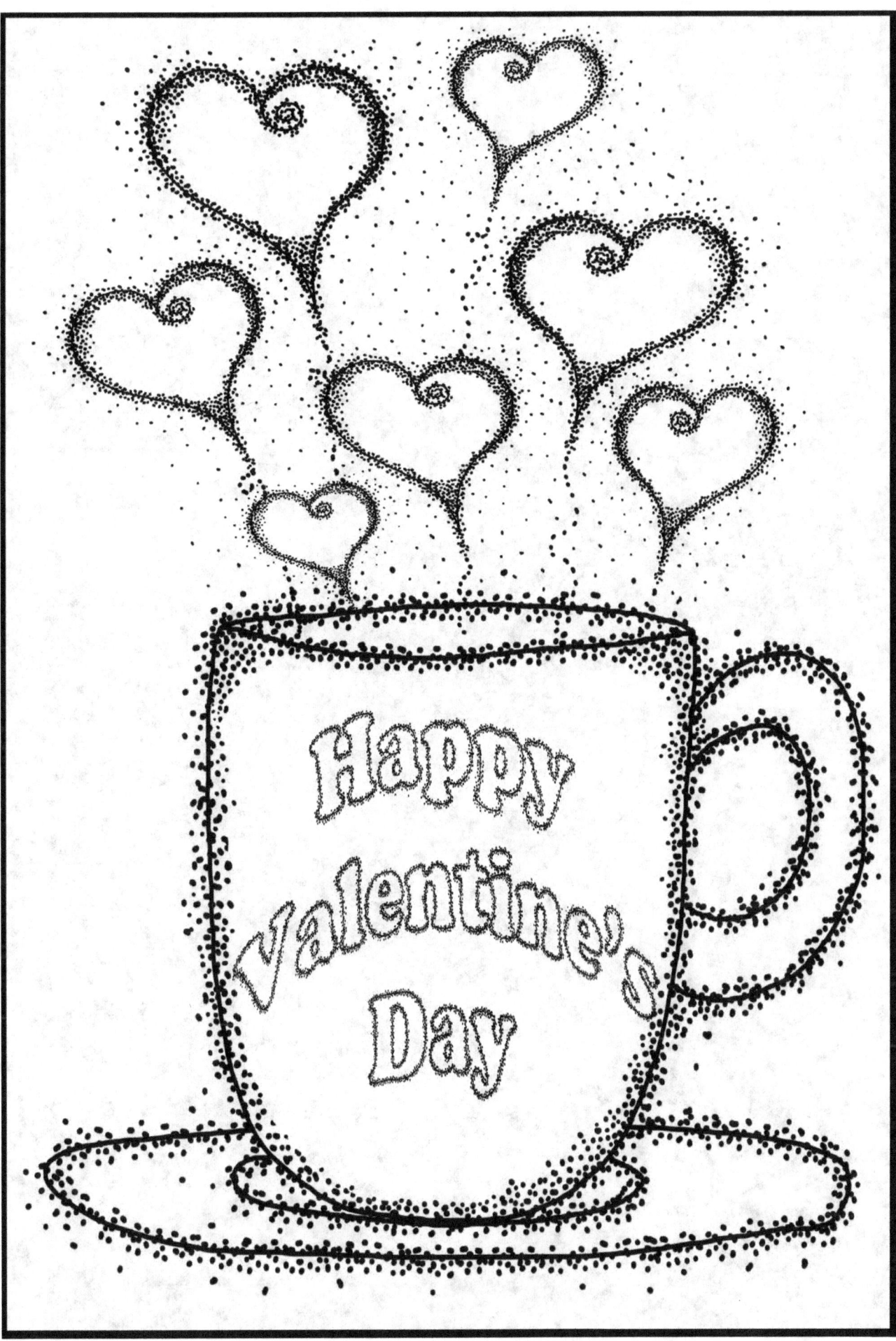

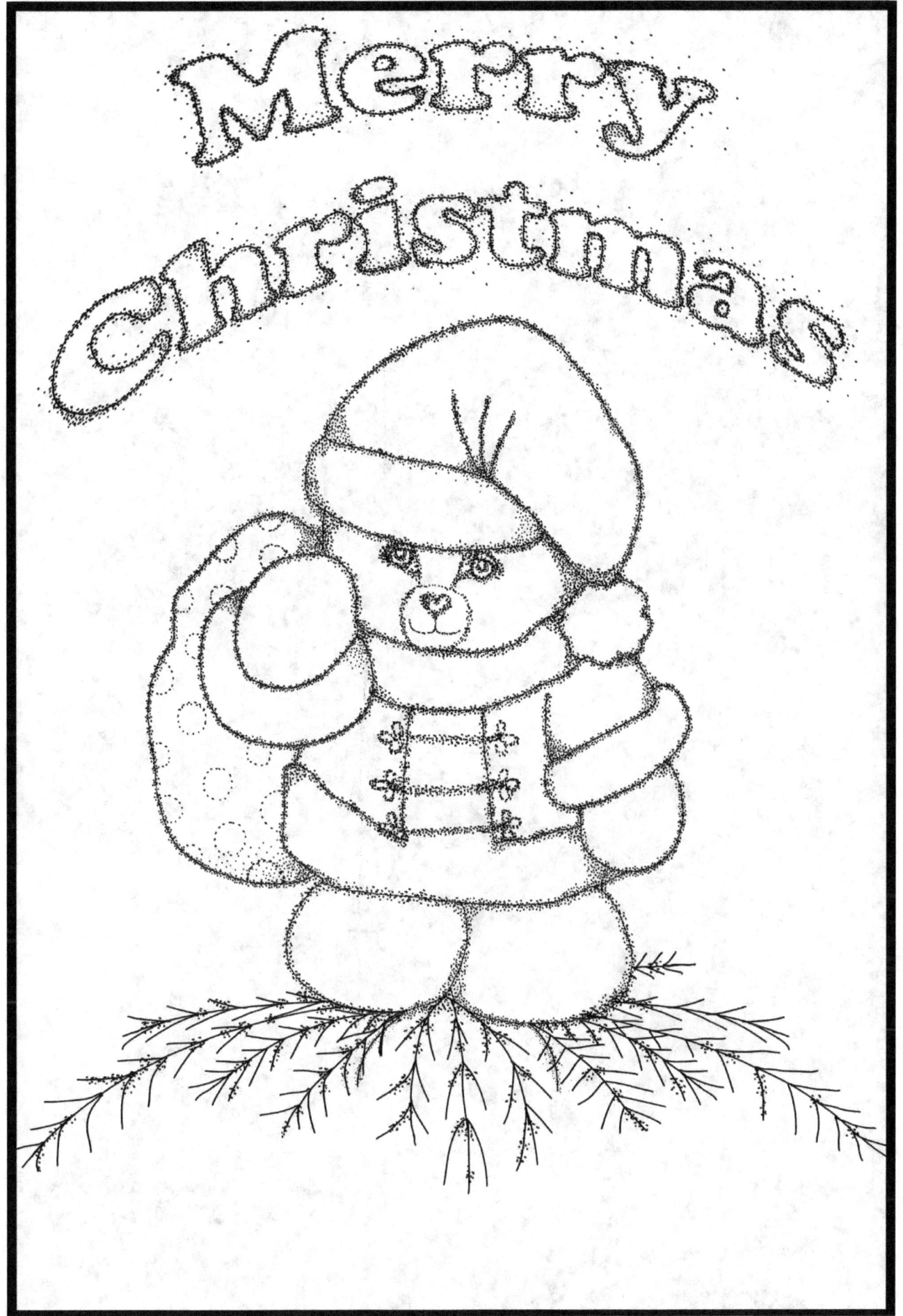

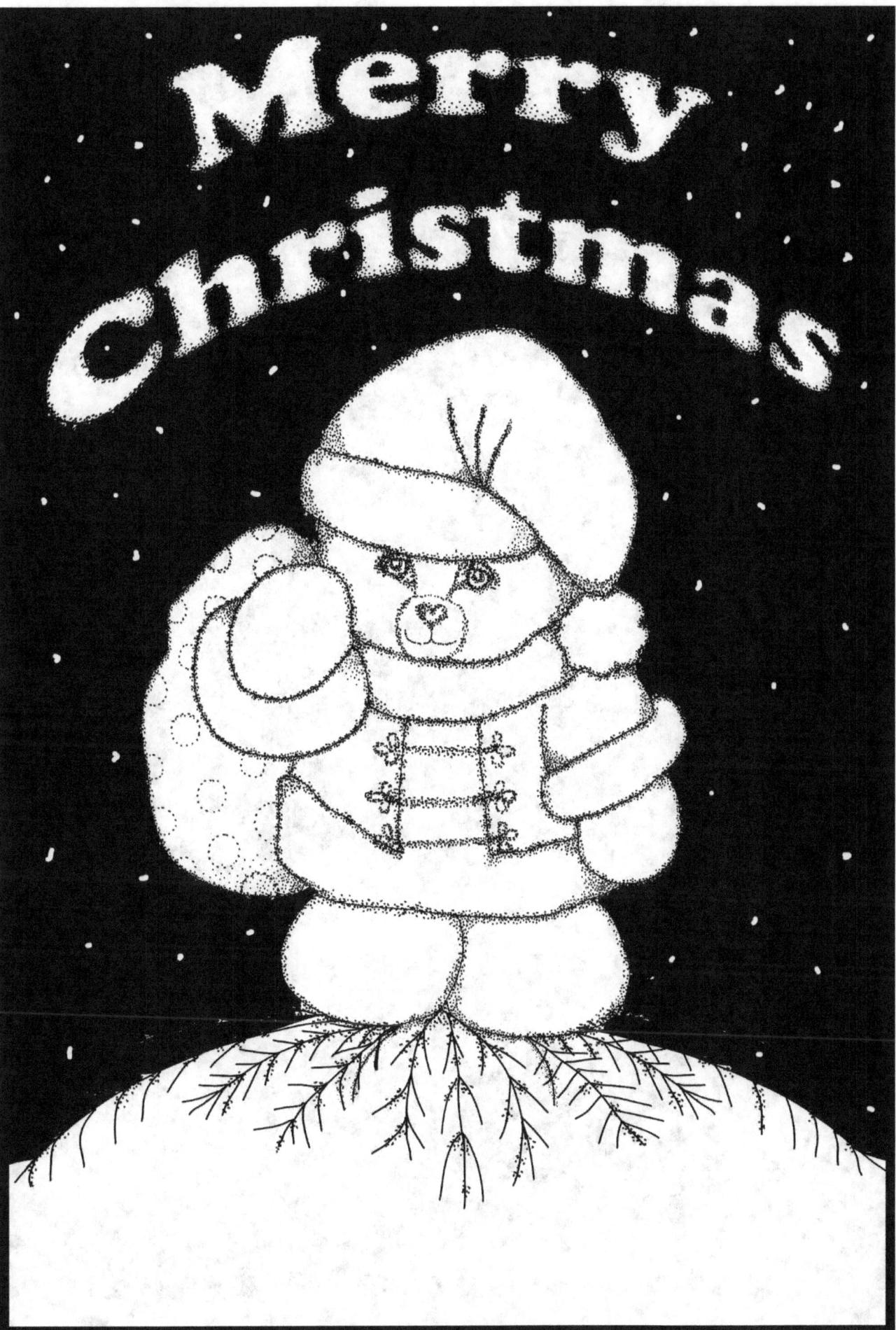

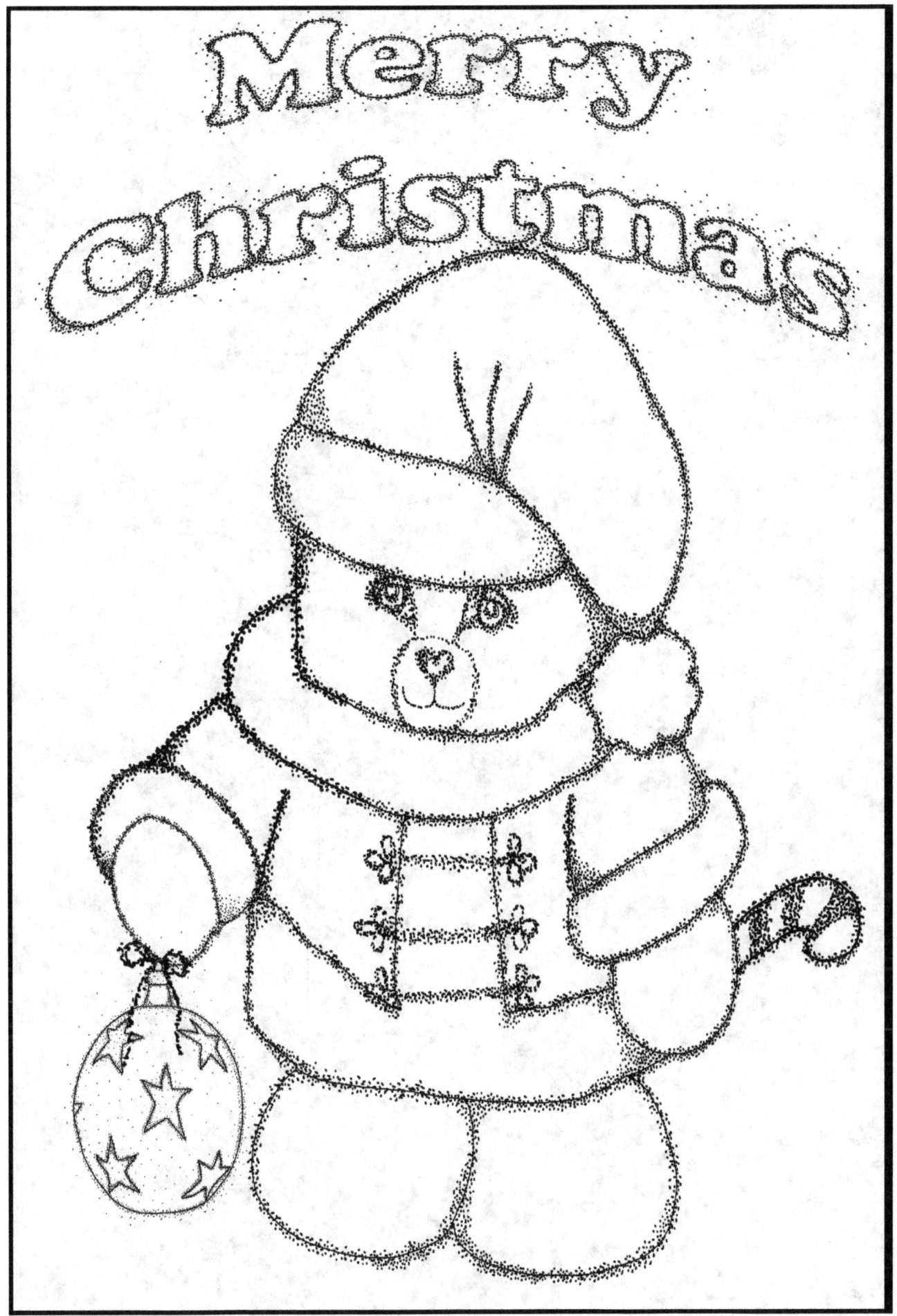

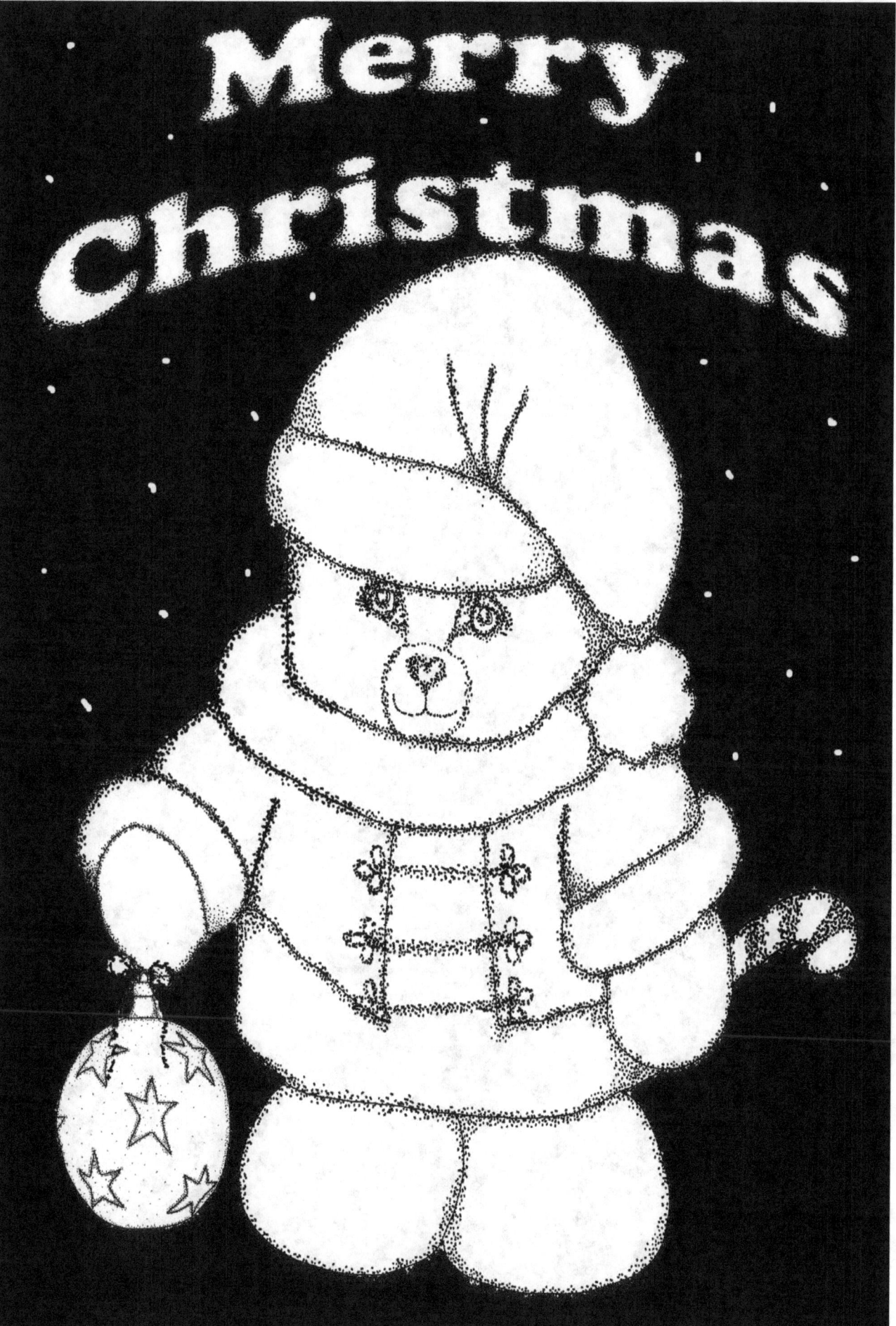

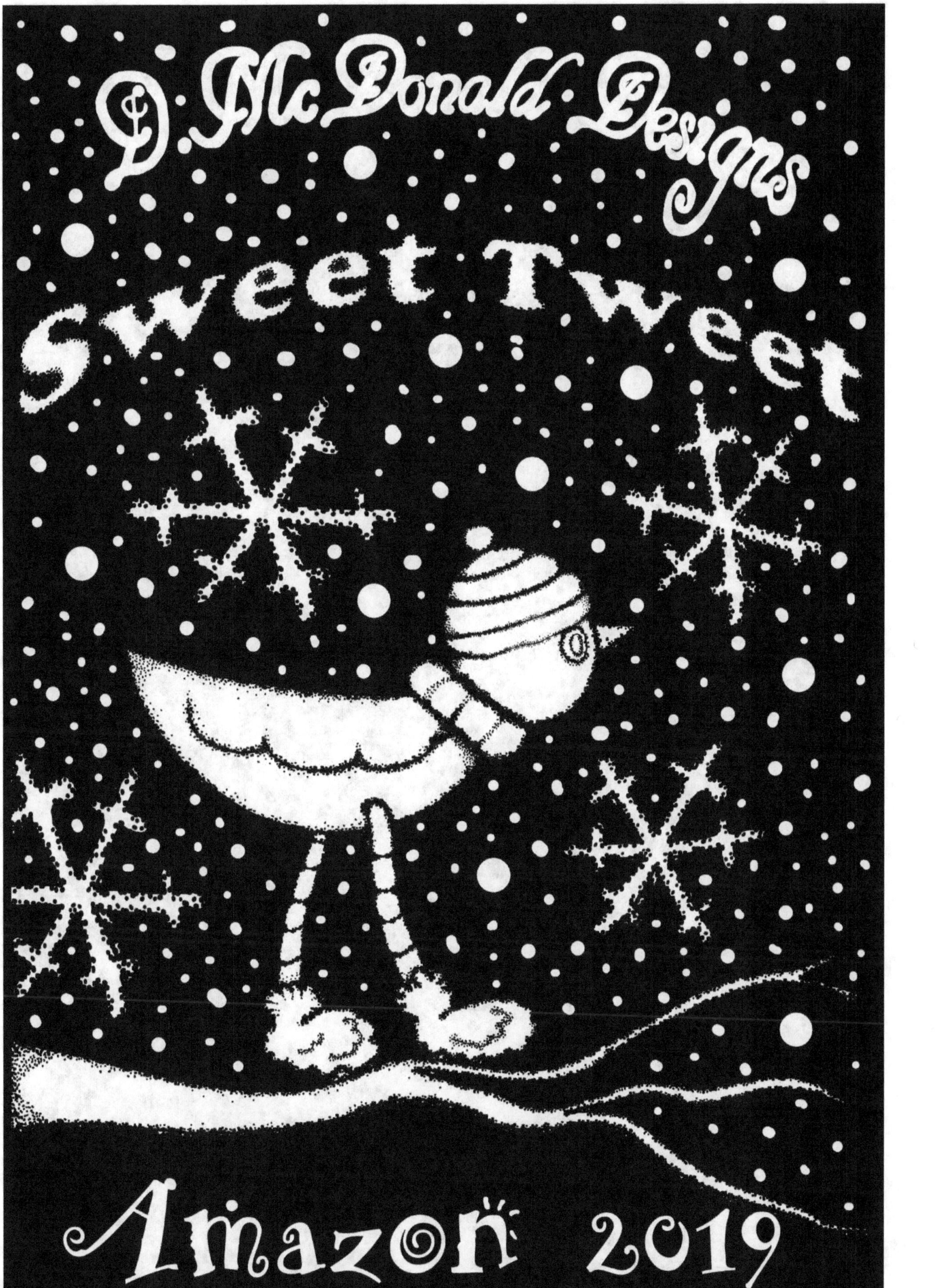
D McDonald Designs
Sweet Tweet
Amazon 2019

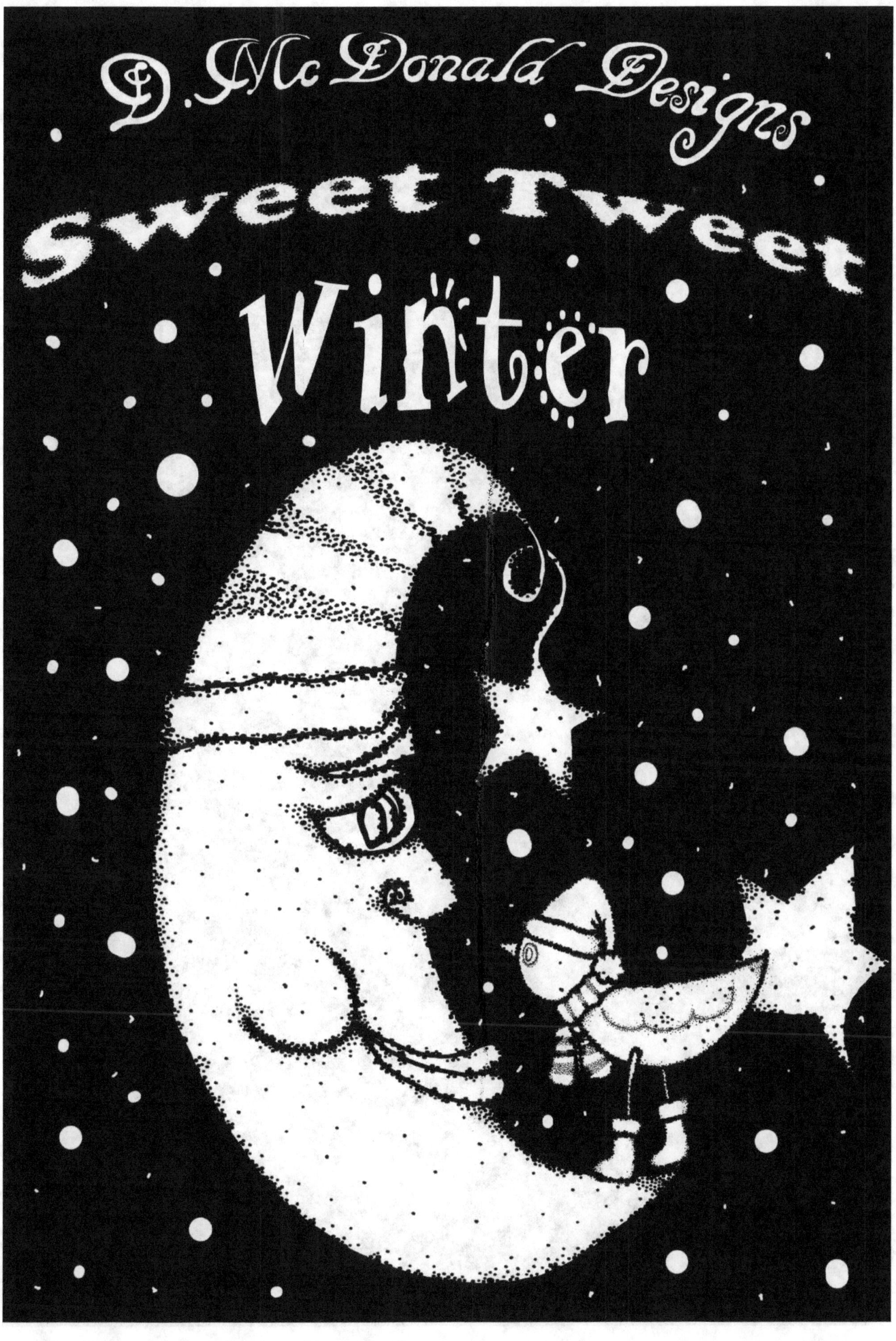
D.J.McDonald Designs
Sweet Tweet
Winter

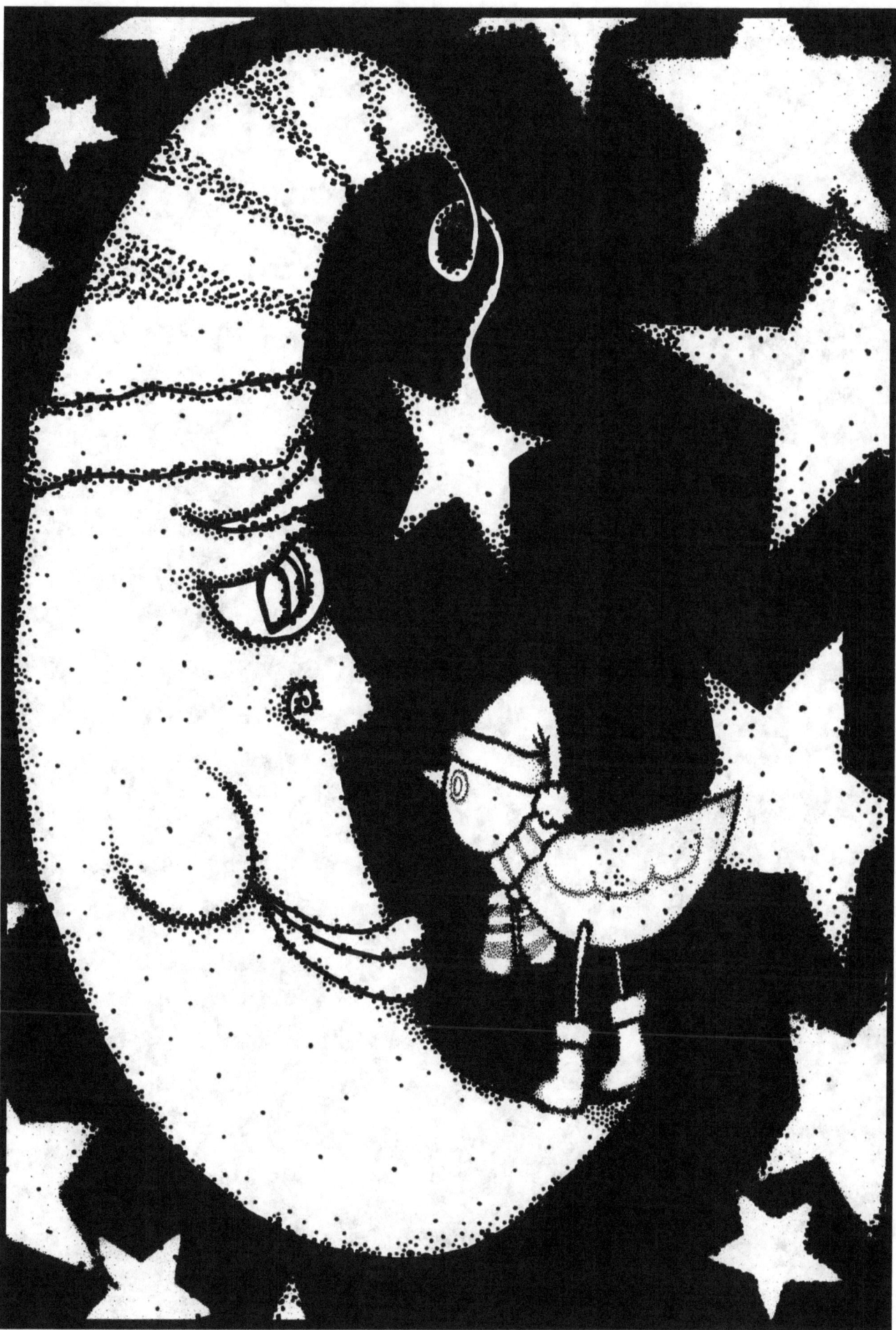

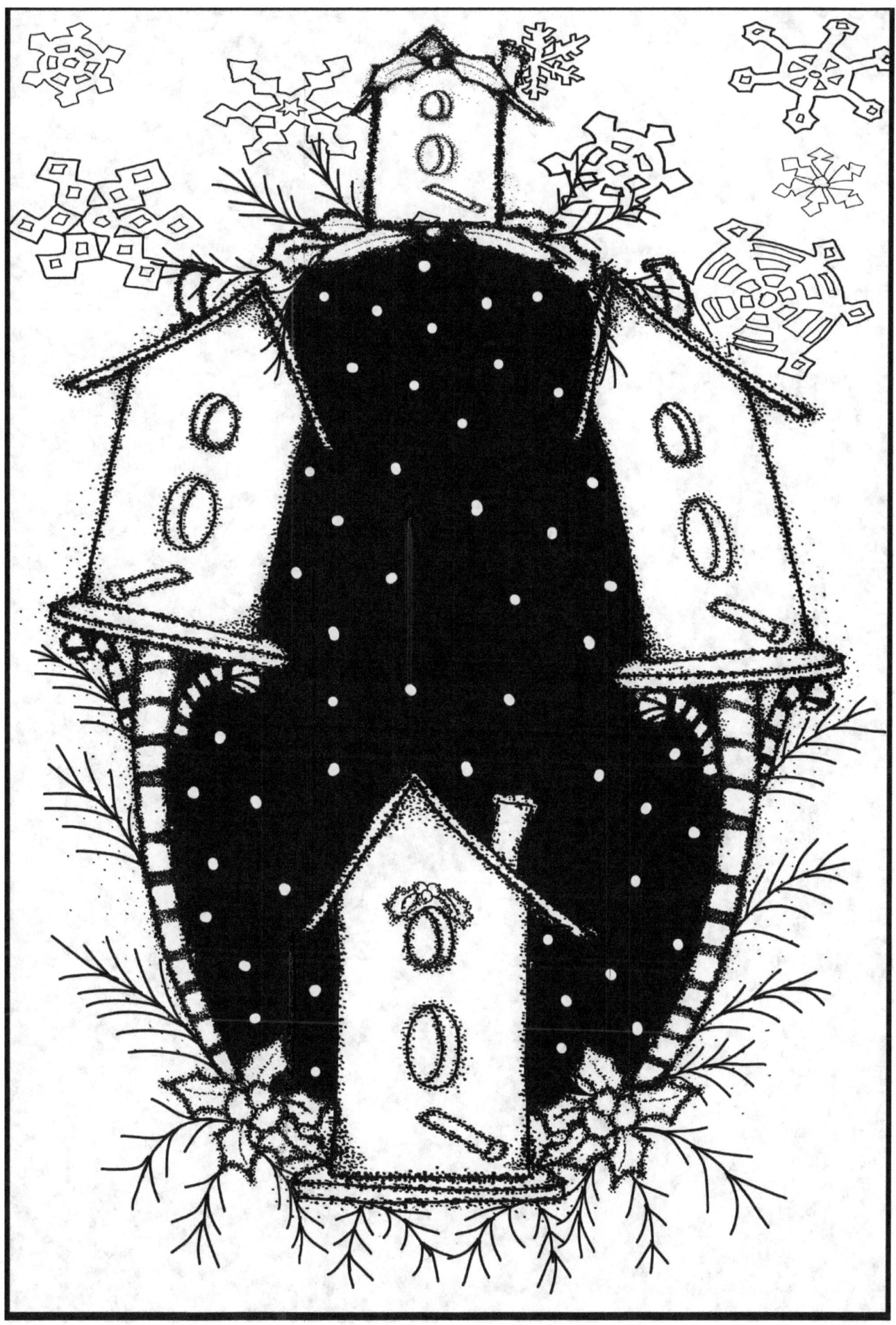

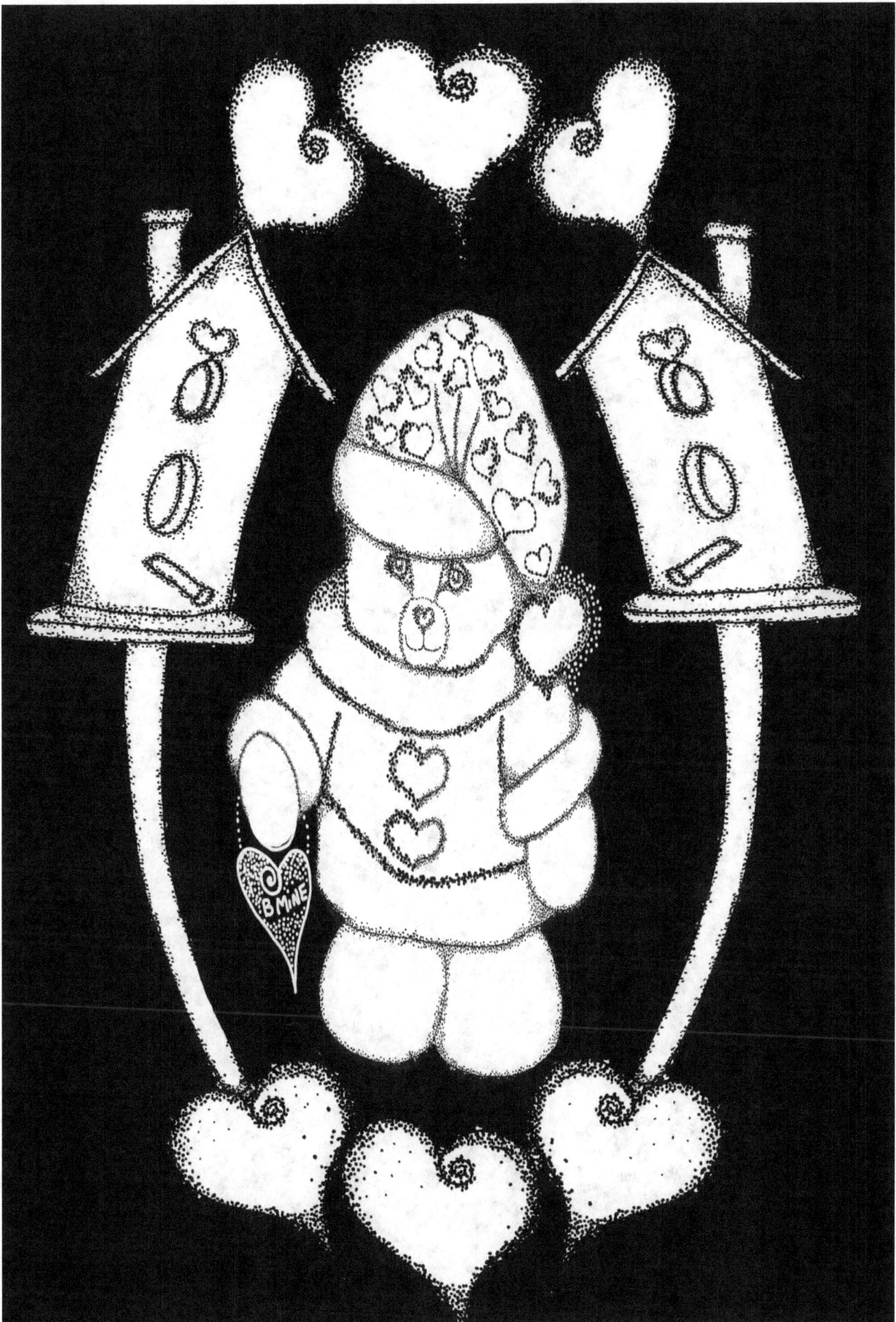

www.ingramcontent.com/pod-product-compliance
Lightning Source LLC
Chambersburg PA
CBHW081738220526
45468CB00008B/2149